The Joy of
Thinking Big

The Joy of Thinking Big

Becoming a Genius in No Time Flat

ERNIE J. ZELINSKI

Ten Speed Press
Berkeley, California

Ten Speed Press
P.O. Box 7123
Berkeley, CA 94707

Published in Canada in 1994 as *The Joy of Not Knowing It All* by Visions International Publishing. Published in Korean in 1997 as *The Joy of Not Knowing It All* by Joong-Ang Daily News, Seoul, South Korea.

Cover design by Vern Busby and Toni Tajima.
Text design by Jeff Brandenburg/ImageComp.
Original illustrations by Vern Busby.
"Calvin and Hobbes" by Bill Watterson (pp. 7, 10, 32, 154, and 165), copyright © Watterson; "Bizarro" by Dan Piraro (pp. 147 and 174); and "Mr. Boffo" by Joe Martin (p. 95), are reprinted with permission of Universal Press Syndicate; all rights reserved. "Beetle Bailey" by Mort Walker (p. 15) is reprinted with special permission of King Features Syndicate. "Frank & Ernest" by Bob Thaves (p. 126) is reprinted with permission of Newspaper Enterprise Association. The Glasbergen cartoons (pp. 101, 110) are reprinted with permission of *Going Bonkers* magazine, Palm Beach, Florida.

Library of Congress Cataloging-in-Publication Data

Zelinski, Ernie J. (Ernie John), 1949–
    [Joy of not knowing it all]
    The joy of thinking big : becoming a genius in no time flat / Ernie J. Zelinski.
      p.   cm.
    Previously published as: The joy of not knowing it all.
    Includes bibliographical references.
    ISBN 0–89815–980–6 (alk. paper)
    1. Creative thinking.   2. Creative ability.   I. Title.
BF408.Z45   1997
153.3'5—DC21
                                97–31298
                                     CIP

Printed in the United States of America

First printing, 1998

1 2 3 4 5 6 7 8 9 10 — 02 01 00 99 98

To all the creative people throughout the ages who have been willing to risk, be different, challenge the status quo, ruffle a few feathers, and in the process, truly make a big difference in this world.

Contents

Preface

The Paradox of Creativity

A resource vital to modern-day business and personal success remains largely unused by the majority of us. This resource is more powerful and plentiful than financial reserves, physical assets, supportive friends, and loyal customers. The resource is our personal creativity; a renewable and inexpensive-to-develop resource. If used properly, our creativity can become our most important asset for achieving personal success.

Creativity is a resource we all possess; however, few of us use it well. The reasons are many: Some of us are unaware of the power of creativity. Some of us are aware of it, but do not know how to use it. Some of us use our creativity, but not as often as we should. Some of us are afraid to use it. Only a small minority of us have come close to tapping the full benefits of this personal skill.

This book is about how to enhance your creativity. How do I know that your creativity has to be enhanced? I don't. However, I have made a few interesting observations over the last few years, while teaching creativity. A strange paradox is evident; the people and organizations who most need to have their creative abilities enhanced are the most resistant to participating in any related learning activities.

> Beware when the great God lets loose a thinker on this planet.
> — *Ralph Waldo Emerson*

The opposite is true with creative people and innovative companies. They are most eager to look at new ways and not-so-new ways to stimulate their creativity. A good example is Grant Lovig and his staff at Company's Coming Publishing. They helped Grant's mother, Jean Paré, market over ten million of her *Company's Coming* cookbooks in a Canadian industry where five thousand copies is considered a bestseller. With their phenomenal success in innovative marketing, the staff at Company's Coming is one of the last groups I know who need a lesson in creativity and innovation. Nevertheless, Grant and his staff were most receptive to a creativity seminar that I conducted for them. Many people and companies need to know more about how to be more innovative. They could benefit immensely from improving their creative thinking; however, there is a catch-22. Because they don't understand the benefits of creativity, they will never take steps to learn about it. Of course, they will never understand the benefits until they take steps to learn about it.

Why do the highly creative individuals of this world spend time on enhancing their creativity? The enhancement of creativity is like most self-improvement activities. Self-improvement is not a destination; it is a journey. Even creative people in this world have to practice and remind themselves what makes people creative and successful. The thing that separates successful people from the less successful ones is that the successful people are always taking part in interesting journeys of learning. They are doers. They continually strive for self-improvement. The less successful are not doers. They may be interested in destinations but resist making the necessary journeys. Without journeys come no new destinations.

> Nothing is more dangerous than an idea, when it's the only one we have.
>
> — *Émile Chartier*

The journey of learning helps us get to new and exciting places. My wish is that all participants in my seminars and readers of my books find themselves on a worthwhile journey like the wonderful one I have had in learning about creativity and teaching it to others. Bon voyage.

Introduction to Creativity and Innovation

So What's the Point of Being Creative?

I hope this book will open up a new way of life for you rather than just give you a technique or two to add to those you already use. If you are determined to apply creativity to your work and play, your life will change immensely, no matter what your age, background, sex, marital status, or occupation.

In my seminar presentations to professional associations I often say, "A creative businessperson is an entrepreneur; a creative speaker is an orator; a creative welder is a sculptor; a creative engineer is an inventor, and a creative accountant is . . . well, I guess a creative accountant is an embezzler." Of course, I am only kidding. Accountants don't have to be embezzlers to be creative. Even accountants who have rigid guidelines to abide by in their pure accounting work still have much opportunity to be creative in many other aspects of their everyday work.

> Everyone is a genius at least once a year; a real genius has his original ideas closer together.
> — G. C. Lichtenberg

The same applies to you. Whether you are a nurse, school teacher, janitor, clerical worker, homemaker, manager, truck driver, or bartender, you can find areas in your work in which you can be more creative. Note, if you are employed in an area such as advertising, you are fooling yourself if you think everyone in your field is naturally creative and can't benefit from creativity training. In my seminars several people in advertising have commented how uncreative many people in their field are, and recently the *Toronto Star* published an article about the lack of creativity in advertising. You can also profit from creativity at play. Being creative is much more important for handling leisure activities than is having lots of money. I must warn you that if you haven't developed the ability to be creative in your leisure time by the time you retire, you will feel the life of leisure is the biggest rip-off since the last time you got conned into buying the Brooklyn Bridge or swampland in Florida.

If you don't think you have to be creative to succeed in today's world, think again, and again, and again. (I am just trying to get your mind all revved up for what's ahead.) The most successful people in the new millennium will be highly creative people who are flexible thinkers and can deal with rapid change.

More and more businesspeople and government leaders are focusing on hiring highly creative employees, so their organizations can survive in the global economy and the rapidly changing world. Educational institutions are seeing a need to teach creativity. Creativity is showing up in programs right from kindergarten up to graduate programs at universities. For example, several business departments at American universities, such as the Graduate School of Business at Stanford University, have courses in enhancing personal creativity.

What's a cleb? It's a belc spelled backwards.

Creativity is the organization's competitive edge in today's rapidly changing world. It is the special talent that develops the right market segment. It is the ability that turns a crisis into an opportunity. It is the insight that recognizes a better and cheaper way to produce the company's existing product. It is innovation that helps a business prosper while others fail.

The successful corporations in the immediate future will be the most innovative ones. Creativity precedes innovation. Innovation can only happen if organizations have highly creative employees. If you want to be a successful employee or entrepreneur, you will have to be one of these highly creative people.

Exercise I-1. Creativity and You

1. Give a brief definition of creativity.

2. How can you profit from creativity in your career?

3. How can you profit from creativity in your personal life?

4. When was the last time you were creative? How?
   - Today:
   - Yesterday:
   - Last week:
   - Last month or before:

5. What inspires you to be creative?

6. In what type of environment are you most creative?

7. What principles do you consider important for becoming more creative?

Creativity Is Having Your Cake and Eating It Too

Just what is creativity? Posing this question always results in a number of interesting definitions. Here are some answers typical of those that I receive from the participants in my seminars:

- Creativity is being different.
- Creativity is the Mona Lisa.
- Creativity is thinking differently.
- Creativity is living happily unemployed.
- Creativity is being a genius.
- Creativity is having your cake and eating it too.
- Creativity is wanting to know.
- Creativity is being able to solve problems.
- Creativity is something children are good at.
- Creativity is playing a prank on a friend.
- Creativity is being unreasonable and crazy.
- Creativity is the ability to enjoy almost everything in life.
- Creativity is daydreaming at work without being caught.
- Creativity is being able to generate many options to just about any problem.

These are just a few of the many different definitions that are possible for creativity. All of the definitions represent some essence of the creative process. Even "creativity is being a genius" is appropriate since we all have some genius in us. Creativity means different things to different people. Creativity is an experience, and all our experiences are somewhat different. The myriad of definitions reflects the many sides of creativity.

My personal definition is "creativity is the joy of not knowing it all." "The joy of not knowing it all" refers to the realization that we seldom if ever have all the answers; we always have the ability to generate more solutions to just about any problem. Being creative is being able to see or imagine a great deal of opportunity in life's problems. Creativity is having many options. This book is about how to enhance our ability to generate opportunity and options that we would not otherwise generate.

In assigning a general definition to creativity, we can say that creativity is the ability to think or do something new. By new we do not mean new to all the world. We mean new to the person who is thinking or doing it. The ability to come up with something new is generally not a function of heredity, nor is it a function of an extremely high education.

Creativity can be learned. There is no magic associated with the ability to see more and come up with new ideas or solutions. Creativity is a skill that can be developed by just about everyone. It is a thinking skill, not difficult to master. But no matter what our level of mastery, creativity will remain a skill that we can always improve. All being creative involves is awareness of some basic principles and then use of these principles in our lives. Both organizations and individuals may gain many benefits from practicing creativity.

The ultimate objective is to help you discover the genius within you. Then you can have your cake and eat it too. How? It's actually quite easy — just get yourself two cakes.

Seventeen (More or Less) Principles of Creativity

Following are seventeen principles (more or less) that I consider basic for being creative at work or play. I don't claim that these are the only available principles for enhancing your creativity. Other principles and techniques exist. The objective is to enhance your ability to see and generate more options by using as many techniques as possible.

Seventeen Principles of Creativity

- Choose to be creative.
- Look for many solutions.
- Write down all your ideas.
- Fully analyze your ideas.
- Define your goals.
- See problems as opportunities.
- Look for the obvious.
- Take risks.
- Dare to be different.
- Be unreasonable.
- Have fun and be foolish.
- Be spontaneous.
- Be in the now.
- Practice divergent thinking.
- Challenge rules and assumptions.
- Delay your decision.
- Be persistent.

> Creativity is the sudden cessation of stupidity.
>
> — *Dr. E. Land (Inventor of the Polaroid Camera)*

Don't Forget the Problem

Using the above principles of creativity to solve your problems will enhance both your career and personal life. In applying these principles of creativity to any problem, of course, you must first identify the problem.

You may think that your problem is your unhappiness, because you don't have a marriage partner, when your actual problem is you are unhappy due to a lack of self-esteem. Generating a lot of solutions for finding a marriage partner may result in your finding a partner, but your unhappiness will persist because you haven't solved the real problem of having low self-esteem. If you define the problem correctly as unhappiness due to lack of self-esteem, then your solutions will be more effective in solving the issue of unhappiness.

> The uncreative mind can spot wrong answers, but it takes a creative mind to spot wrong questions.
>
> — Anthony Jay

Identifying the problem is crucial. Let me give you an example. At a conference for young adults involved with Junior Achievement, at the Banff Springs Hotel, I was all set to make my keynote speech. The hotel sound technician wouldn't let me proceed, due to the apparent feedback on the sound system. He asked me to turn off my clip-on cordless microphone, which I did. The sound persisted, so he asked me to turn off the power supply, which I also did. Fifteen minutes after my speech was supposed to commence, the technician was going crazy, still trying to figure out what was causing the feedback. Much to his astonishment, turning off the power for both the main sound system and the cordless microphone hadn't helped.

> It isn't that they can't see the solution. It is that they can't see the problem.
>
> — G. K. Chesterton

That is when I thought, "Have we identified the problem correctly?" I then walked to the back of the auditorium, and there was the problem staring me in the face. Four high-school students were all rubbing the rims of their water glasses with their forefingers and creating the highpitched noise you have undoubtedly heard before, which sounds similar to the feedback that comes from sound systems. Because we hadn't identified the problem correctly, we didn't stand a chance of coming up with an effective solution. We still might have been there trying to figure out what was causing the "feedback" problem if the problem hadn't been correctly identified.

Four Stages of Creativity

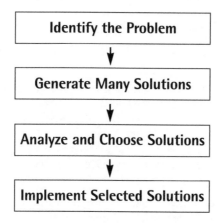

Let me give you another example of how I almost missed identifying the right problem. This could have cost me a lot of time and money and produced few, if any, results. When I was starting out in the seminar business, I sent out a brochure to company presidents and human resource managers. I wasn't getting much response from this brochure about my creativity seminars, so I decided my problem was an uninteresting brochure. Before I spent money on an expensive brochure, I decided to kick around and study my problem. Eventually I realized my problem actually was how to get the attention and interest of the decision makers of organizations. After realizing what my problem was, I asked this dumb question: Do I even need a brochure? No! Instead of spending more money on another brochure, which most people would have thrown away unread because of all the brochures they get, I created an exercise and sent it out in a letter. The following letter was used; it was twenty times as effective as mailing an expensive brochure.

> A problem well stated is
> a problem half solved.
> — *Charles F. Kettering*

Mr. Anderson, General Manager
CFFC Radio Network
Vancouver, BC

Dear Mr. Anderson:

I would like you to consider something very important. How innovative
are your key employees? They may not be as innovative as you would like
them to be. In this age of business the most imaginative organizations
are the ones turning ideas into big dollars. This means your company has
to be creative or be left behind. Your employees should be innovative in
generating new services, increasing productivity, finding fresh ways of promoting products, and developing new market segments.

Here is an interesting way to find out how innovative your employees
really are. Ask them to do this challenging exercise.

Exercise: What do a bed, book, and beer have in common?

Highly innovative employees will have no problem in thinking of at least
twenty answers to this exercise. Many employees will think of only five or
so. Some will stop after one or two. Just think of the missed business
opportunities if there are more than twenty new opportunities available
and your employees think of only one or two.

In the next few days I will forward a list of thirty answers to this exercise
(generated by one person). I will also forward details of how we can
enhance the creativity of all your employees, even those who are already
highly innovative.

Sincerely,

Ernie J. Zelinski

So don't forget to spend a little, or even a lot, of time just analyzing
what your problem is. What's the use of generating a lot of brilliant
solutions if you don't have a clue what the problem is? After you have
identified your problem, generated many solutions, and analyzed your
solutions, you will be ready to implement your selected solutions. In the
implementation stage, you will invariably discover that another problem arises. Don't despair. This is an opportunity to be creative again by
using the seventeen principles of creativity in accordance with the four
stages shown above.

The Most Important Creativity Principle

Creativity is an important force to help us be truly alive. The highly creative individual is constantly discovering new events, finding new ways of doing things, and arriving at new insights in life. Creative people are flexible people. Taoism extols the virtue of flexibility. What survives on earth is what effortlessly adapts to the changing environment and changing circumstances. Your flexibility will help you change plans in midstream, respond to the unexpected at a moment's notice, or rearrange a schedule without experiencing emotional turmoil.

> To create you must first destroy.
> — *Pablo Picasso*

So, start being more creative immediately. You must constantly remember how crucial imagination is for success in life. In any field of endeavor, imaginative people are the most successful over the long term. They see opportunity where others see insurmountable problems. Creative individuals take action in a difficult situation, instead of complaining about it. Utilizing one's creativity determines a great range of life's successes, including acquiring promotions, experiencing happiness, developing meaningful relationships, and maintaining physical and emotional health.

By the way, there is one more creativity principle in addition to the seventeen previously mentioned. The last principle is the most important: Ignore all the principles of creativity that don't apply in your life. Who says there has to be a right or wrong way to be creative? Other techniques exist. Your objective is to enhance your ability to see and generate more options in your life by using as many techniques as possible.

How to Be Creative and Write Graffiti

To Be More Creative, Forget What You Know

Let us begin this chapter with the following exercise.

Exercise 1-1. Columbus and the Eggheads

At the royal court in Spain, Christopher Columbus asked the court attendants if they could get an egg to stand on its end. They tried and could not do it. They thought it was impossible.

Columbus then said he could do it. The attendants bet him he could not. Columbus then proceeded to make the egg stand on its end. He collected his bet, much to the frustration of the attendants.

What do you think Columbus did?

> Happiness lies in the joy of achievement and the thrill of creative effort.
>
> — *Franklin D. Roosevelt*

Without any prior knowledge of the preceding exercise, did you generate some good new ideas for solving it ? (See Chapter Notes, page 8, for solutions.) Were there new thoughts in your solutions or were you searching for something that you already know? Keep this in mind: Creativity goes beyond what you already know. What you know is just knowledge.

Knowledge is not creativity; creativity transcends knowledge. This is an important distinction. Many people feel that grasping and remembering a myriad of facts and figures will give them the edge in life. This may give them the edge in trivial pursuits; however, having the edge in the important things in life is dependent on having the creative edge. The ability to think in new ways is much more important than the ability to remember what team won the Stanley Cup or which Fortune 500 company had the highest profits last year.

> What's on your mind, if you will allow the overstatement?
> — *Fred Allen*

To be more creative, try setting aside your knowledge. You may have to challenge, and even forget, what you know. The distinction between creativity and knowledge is important. Stephen Leacock said, "Personally, I would sooner have written *Alice in Wonderland* than the whole *Encyclopedia Britannica*." Albert Einstein was emphasizing the same point when he said, "Imagination is much more important than knowledge." What Leacock and Einstein were saying is that imagination transcends knowledge.

> Very few people do anything creative after the age of thirty-five. The reason is that very few people do anything creative before the age of thirty-five.
> — *Joel Hildebrand*

We have broadly defined creativity as the ability to come up with something new. How new were your ideas on how to stand an egg on its end? Knowledge of old ways is valuable; nevertheless, we must often look for fresh ideas if we are to find more effective solutions. Innovative thinking is approaching life's situations and problems in new ways so that they are handled with greater ease.

New approaches are possible for just about anything. Abraham Maslow stated that a truly good soup can be as creative as a great painting or a marvelous symphony. Creativity can be found in music, painting, cooking, engineering, carpentry, accounting, law, economics, leisure, and sports. It has been with us through the ages and will continue to play an even more important role in our future development.

How Creative Are You Really?

Whether at work or play, you can be more creative. So the question is: How creative are you really? I would like you to do exercise 1-2, which is the one I used in my letter shown on page xx.

Exercise 1-2.

What do a bed, book, and beer have in common?

Note that highly creative individuals will have no problem in thinking of at least twenty answers to this exercise. Many people will think of only five or so. Some will stop after one or two. If you stopped after one or two solutions to this exercise, do you also stop after one or two solutions to your everyday problems at work or play?

If you thought of only one or two solutions to this exercise, you didn't put enough effort into solving it. After you look at my solutions (see Chapter Notes, page 8), you will see that the number of solutions to this exercise, as to many problems in life, is endless. You are missing out on many opportunities in your life if you are thinking of only one or two solutions when there are many solutions or, in some cases, even an endless number.

What a bed, book, and beer have in common is this crackpot Zelinski has used all of them in a stupid exercise.

How you can use creativity at work and play is unlimited as well. Creativity can be found in every facet of human life. From the graffiti and the creative lawyer written about on the following pages to the examples cited in subsequent chapters, you will see many ways to use creativity for enhancing your life. Some of the benefits you will get from making the effort to be more creative include increased self-esteem, personal growth, more enthusiasm for solving problems, increased confidence to deal with new challenges, and different perspectives toward work and personal life.

Creativity Put in a Can
(The Creativity of Good Graffiti)

God is dead.
—Nietzsche
Nietzsche is dead.
—God

PREPARE TO MEET GOD!
(JACKET AND TIE, NO JEANS)

We should hang all the extremists!

Eve was framed

HUMPTY DUMPTY WAS PUSHED

DEATH IS NATURE'S WAY OF
TELLING YOU TO SLOW DOWN

JESUS SAVES!
(BUT GRETZKY TIPS IN THE REBOUND)

POINT OF VIEW IS RELATIVE
(said Picasso to Einstein)

Reality is for those who
cannot handle booze or drugs

Bad spellers of
the world, Untie!

Mickey Mouse is a rat!

Drink wet cement and get really stoned

I'd give my left arm to
be ambidextrous

PLEASE DO NOT FLUSH WHILE TRAIN IS IN STATION
(EXCEPT IN PITTSBURGH!)

Sex education is interesting
but I never get any homework

Isaac Newton was right!
This is the center of Graffiti.

I can't stand
intolerance

Roy Rogers was trigger happy

I'M SCHIZOPHRENIC.
(So am I. That makes four of us.)

Power corrupts. Absolute power is even more fun.

DON'T LOOK UP HERE! THE JOKE IS IN YOUR HANDS!
(written above a urinal)

My dad says they don't work.
(written on contraceptive vending machine)

Celibacy is not an
inherited characteristic

Graffiti's days are numbered
The writing is on the wall.

BILL STICKERS WILL BE PROSECUTED.
(Bill Stickers is innocent. OK!)

Even Lawyers Can Be Creative

The true account of the court action described below shows that lawyers, like everyone else, can be very creative.

On November 23, 1917, a statement of claim was filed in the District Court of Battleford by the plaintiffs, H. C. Humphrey and H. G. Chard, for damages to their female pig allegedly caused by a male pig owned by the defendant, Joseph Odishaw. The statement of claim, in part, read:

> I can't do no literary work for the rest of this year because I'm meditating another lawsuit and looking around for a defendant.
>
> — *Mark Twain*

> That on or about the 4th day of November, 1917, a boar, the property of the Defendant, was allowed by the Defendant to run at large contrary to the provisions of the said By-Law and the said boar broke and entered the lands of the Plaintiffs, being the lands above described, on or about the 4th day of November, 1917, and served a valuable sow of the Plaintiffs and the said sow became in pig to the great damage of the Plaintiffs.
>
> The Plaintiffs therefore claim: $200.00 damages, and the cost of this action.

On January 14, 1918, the defendant's lawyer, A.M. Panton K.C., of the city of North Battleford filed a statement of defense. The third alternative in the statement of defense reads:

> In the alternative the Defendant says if his boar entered the close of the plaintiffs and had intercourse with the said sow that he did so at the solicitation of the said sow and that the said boar merely yielded to her blandishments and that she was solely guilty of the behavior complained of or is at least in "pari delicto" with the said boar and that her masters the said Plaintiffs are guilty of an offence against the public morals in keeping a sow of such depraved habits to corrupt the morals of the neighborhood.
>
> The Defendant waives his right to a counter-claim against the Plaintiffs for lowering the vital powers of the said boar upon which the Defendant might properly look for sustenance.
>
> The Defendant therefore claims that this action be dismissed against him with costs.

Incidentally, there was no record of a trial or judgment in this case. Apparently, the case was dropped or dismissed.

Does It Matter If Your Brain Is Tilted Left or Right?

Creative thinking can be broken down into two types. Both types are important for the creative process.

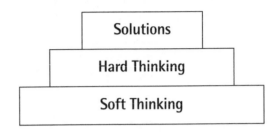

Soft Thinking is the mode of thinking that most of us can improve. Many artists and musicians are good at this type of thinking. School systems and organizations normally frown at us if we think softly.

So you're an artist. You guys have some sort of right-brain tilt, don't you?

Soft thinking requires us to be flexible and random. It involves the unreasonable and the nonjudgmental. Humor and playfulness originate from soft thinking. This mode of thinking is valuable for generating a large number of ideas. Researchers say soft thinking is performed by the right side of our brains. Generally speaking, for problem solving soft thinking should be done before any hard thinking is started.

Hard Thinking is the type of thinking most of us are pretty good at. It is the analytical thinking for which school systems and organizations reward us.

This thinking mode makes us logical and practical. It is what our parents want us to be. Society also prefers us when we are logical and practical.

Hard thinking is needed for analysis of ideas, when we focus on usable solutions to our problems. We use hard thinking to put our plan into action. The left part of the brain is responsible for this thinking mode.

Left Brain	Right Brain
practical	unreasonable
serious	playful
analytical	intuitive
structured	flexible
judgmental	nonjudgmental
orderly	random
Hard Thinking	**Soft Thinking**

Solutions require both thinking processes to have both quality and quantity. However, most of us don't use both styles of thinking effectively. Many of us use mainly the hard-thinking process, whereas some of us utilize mainly the soft-thinking process.

Creative Success = Hard + Soft Thinking

Innovative solutions are dependent on both modes of thinking. First, we should generate many ideas using soft thinking. Then, using hard-thinking processes, we should evaluate the ideas for their merits. Our end result should be several good options for the problem in question.

True creative thinking is a balance between soft and hard thinking, both used at appropriate times. Problem solving mainly through hard thinking isn't effective if there are few ideas with which to work. Similarly, it isn't effective to have generated a lot of ideas via soft thinking and not have properly analyzed and implemented these ideas.

CALVIN AND HOBBES

It is important to note that some researchers frown upon the present trend to label people as either right-brain or left-brain thinkers. The danger is that some people will have an excuse to limit themselves by using the right-brain or left-brain label to say something like, "Well, I am a right-brained thinker and can't be any good at preparing and keeping to a budget."

We all can enhance both our soft- and hard-thinking processes. Researchers have estimated every human brain has about one million, million or 1,000,000,000,000 brain cells. When it comes to creativity, I know some people who appear to be using only about 1,000 of these brain cells and functioning at a modest IQ level of about eighteen.

Don't mess with me, Rivers. I have an IQ of 160.

— *Reggie Jackson*

Jackson, you can't even spell IQ.

— *Micky Rivers*

Indeed, approximately 95 percent of people are dissatisfied with their mental performance. Researchers tell us most people use only 10 percent of their total brains, whether they are left-brain dominant or right-brain dominant. No wonder most of us aren't highly creative; we are wasting about 90 percent of our brains.

Whether we are right-brain dominant or left-brain dominant, we all have billions of underutilized brain cells in both the dominant and the opposite hemispheres of our brains. We all can function better in those areas where we claim we are weak. All it takes is a little effort.

Chapter Notes

Exercise 1-1.
Columbus went into the kitchen and boiled the egg. Then he smashed the end of the egg on the table, causing the egg to stand on its end.

Of course, there are many other ways to stand an egg on its end. In my seminars we have come up with at least twenty. For some of these solutions, see the Appendix, page 177.

Exercise 1-2.
Here are a few of the more obvious and boring solutions. You can hitchhike on these to generate some of your own.

- All are represented by words which start with the letter *b*.
- All have been advertised in magazines.
- All are sold.
- All go through a manufacturing process.

- All three are made for people to use.
- All are represented by words in the English language.
- All are represented by words that are nouns.
- All are represented by words having vowels and consonants.
- All are objects.
- All are represented by words that have one syllable and are singular.

For some more interesting solutions to this exercise see the Appendix, page 177. From the thirty or so solutions I generated, you can see the number of solutions to this exercise is unlimited.

CHAPTER 2

Robbed Blind by the Creativity Bandits

Who Stole Your Creativity?

One evening my rambunctious nephew Cody, five years old at the time, was starting to get on my nerves. So I said to him, "Cody, that's enough; isn't it time you went to sleep? When do you go to sleep?" He looked at me and without hesitation said, "Not in a hundred million years." A little doubtful that he had convinced me, he quickly added, "I don't go to bed until the morning." I was impressed. "Now that's creativity," I thought. Not many adults, if any, could come up with two creative answers like this in such a short time.

CALVIN AND HOBBES

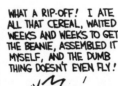

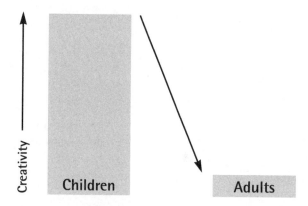

Adults often wonder why young children can have as much fun with the cardboard box a toy came in as with the toy itself. The answer: Children are just more creative than adults. Most adults have become too structured in their thinking, especially toward having fun. They couldn't imagine there are so many interesting ways to enjoy a cardboard box.

Researchers confirm that children are much more creative than adults. What has happened to the creative abilities during those years in between childhood and adulthood? Obviously, we encounter many barriers to expressing our creativity in the world around us.

In fact, it is worse than that. These walls act more like bandits than barriers. By the time we are in midadulthood, nearly all of the creativity we had as children has been taken away by these culprits. *Business Week,* some time ago, reported that an adult of forty is about 2 percent as creative as a child of five.

Who are the responsible culprits who rob us of 98 percent of our creativity by the time we are forty years old? Who can we blame?

The following exercise may give some clues.

Exercise 2-1. To Logo or Not to Logo

You are the new manager of the marketing department of a fairly large company, Trane Computer Systems. Your boss, the general manager of the company, has just come into your office and announced that the company wants to project a new image. She has asked you to personally design a new logo for the company. This new logo has to be done within two weeks.

You realize that the previous marketing manager was a commercial artist who did all the important artwork. You believe that your background in art leaves a lot to be desired. All you know about art is what you took in elementary school. You have not done anything related to art since. No one else in your department claims any more art ability than you do.

How would you respond to this task?

We want all your creativity.

Can't you see I'm forty-five and I don't have any left?

I never let my schooling interfere with my education.
— *Mark Twain*

For the situation in the above exercise, how did you react? Did you give some thought to designing the logo yourself? If you didn't, think why you chose to avoid the task. It could be due to those creativity bandits having robbed you of your willingness to undertake challenging and creative tasks. There are four great brain robbers:

The Four Great Brain Robbers

- Society
- Educational Institutions
- Organizations
- Ourselves

Societal Bandits Demand Your Conformity

If you decided to avoid designing the logo because you have no training in commercial art, you have allowed yourself to be a victim of societal programming. Cultural programming influences us to think that we have to possess a degree or formal training in a certain field to be able to accomplish anything worthwhile in that field. This thinking is absurd. Let us look at a few examples of the many people who accomplished things in fields in which they had no formal training.

- The Coca-Cola logo was designed by an accountant with no training in art.
- Samuel Morse, an artist, invented the telegraph.

Creating a disturbance! Not guilty, Your Honor. I know I'm not creative.

- Robert Campeau, an eighth-grade dropout, amassed a billion-dollar department store empire.
- The Wright brothers invented the airplane. They were bike mechanics and not aeronautical engineers.
- The ballpoint pen was invented by a sculptor.

Society's pressure to have us conform to its programming takes many forms and has many effects. Cultural taboos and traditions are followed to the detriment of new ideas. An overemphasis on competition results in people doing things they would not otherwise do. Similarly, an overemphasis on cooperation results in groupthink. Reason and logic are considered appropriate. Humor, intuition, and fantasy are not appreciated. All of these societal factors rob us of opportunities to be creative.

> Conformity is the jailer of freedom and the enemy of growth.
> — *John F. Kennedy*

Educational Bandits Demand One Right Answer

You may have chosen not to design the logo in exercise 2-1 because you wouldn't know the right way of going about it. Schools teaching us to look for the right way or the one "right" answer is an educational short-coming. There are many right ways for designing logos, as there are many answers to most problems. People leave school systems thinking there is a formula for everything when, in fact, the majority of problems can't be solved with formulas. More creative ways are needed. I have found getting away from the formula to be most effective.

In most school systems reason and logic are overtaught at the expense of other important matters. What the school systems ignore is that business decision making in today's world can't rely solely on reason and logic. Executive officers report using intuition in at least 40 percent of their major decisions. Yet consideration for the intuitive is absent from most school programs, as are the other creativity factors of vision, humor, and enthusiasm.

> In the first place God made idiots. That was for practice. Then he made school boards.
>
> — *Mark Twain*

- Someone once asked the late inventor and philosopher Buckminster Fuller how he came to be a genius. He replied that he wasn't a genius. He stated that he had just not been as damaged by the school system as a lot of other people. He felt that the school system can damage us in many ways.

- Fred Smith, who started the highly successful courier service Federal Express, wrote a paper about the business before he started it. His professor did not think too highly of the idea and gave him a low mark on the paper. Fortunately Fred Smith wasn't influenced by the overintellectual assessment by the professor. His company is now one of the biggest and most innovative courier firms in the world.

Organizational Bandits Demean the Human Spirit

A lot of companies say they are innovative and supportive of creative people. Few really are. Saying the company is innovative sounds nice. These companies say they are innovative because this is the thing to say in this day and age. Looking at many companies' actions reveals a different story. The actions look more like an unconscious attempt to vandalize the creativity shown by the most innovative employees of the organization.

> Education is very admirable but let us not forget that anything worth knowing cannot be taught.
>
> — *Oscar Wilde*

Most of us wouldn't attempt to design the logo in the situation represented in exercise 2-1 because of organizational factors that discourage creative attempts. Being creative involves risk taking. Risk taking is often something we avoid at work. The potential consequences scare us.

BEETLE BAILEY

When a highly creative employee shows up at a company, the company often will not support his or her creativity. Highly innovative people question tradition, challenge the rules, suggest new ways of doing things, tell the truth about things, and appear disruptive to the rest of the employees. The qualities that make these people innovative are usually frowned upon by the company. Attempts are made to transform the highly creative, so they will behave like the less creative employees.

Group norms are protected at the expense of individual effort and ingenuity. Autocratic bosses discourage initiative. The organization sacrifices innovation and creativity so it does not have to deal with the discomfort and disruptiveness necessary for innovation.

Although today's corporations need innovative employees to be highly successful, a lot of organizations end up robbing their employees of the opportunity to be innovative. Success eludes these organizations in the end.

Self Bandits – The Greatest Brain Robbers

We erect many individual barriers that also rob us of our creativity. Avoiding the design of a logo due to our lack of formal training in commercial art may be a result of fear. Fear of failure is one of the more effective robbers of our creativity. Along with fear stand laziness and perception. Both of these can interfere with our willingness to accept the challenge of designing a company logo or undertaking new projects in our lives.

> A man without imagination is like a bird without wings.
> — *Wilhelm Raabe*

Laziness is due to a lack of self-motivation. Motivational experts state that only 10 percent of the North American population is internally or self-motivated. If we only allow ourselves to be externally motivated, we will not undertake the tasks needed to discover and recognize our creative abilities.

We generate many perceptions in our lives, which are not necessarily representative of reality. The perception that we can't design a good logo because we have no formal training is a good example. This perception is false, since most of us who aren't artistic are so because we haven't made the effort to be artistic. Once we make the effort, we all can design a logo.

Perception can distort many of life's realities. Let's look at the following exercises to see how easily our perception can interfere with the true picture.

> It is far safer to know too little than too much.
>
> — Samuel Butler

Perception Can Be Deceiving

Exercise 2-2. Looking at Perception

After you have taken quick glances at the following four figures, write down what you saw on a separate piece of paper.

Opportunity ISNOWHERE

Figure 2-1

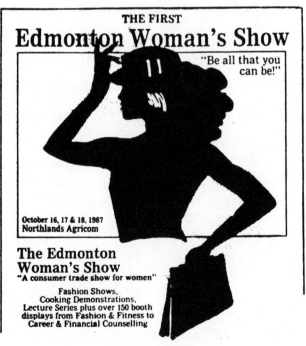

Figure 2-2

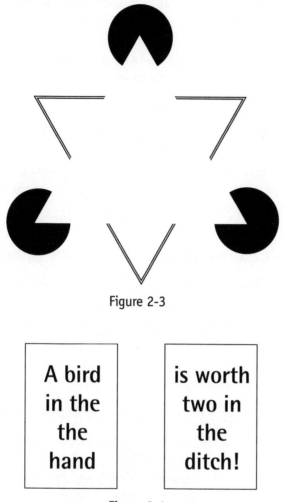

Figure 2-3

| A bird in the the hand | is worth two in the ditch! |

Figure 2-4

The above figures offer some proof that we don't always perceive things as well as we think we do.

If you looked at figure 2-1 and saw only **Opportunity IS NOWHERE,** you haven't seen the opportunity in this figure. This can also stand for **Opportunity IS NOW HERE.**

Figure 2-2 is a photo of an advertisement for a woman's consumer trade show. This is an interesting example of what we can see if we take the time to look. Note there is a silhouette of a man's face in the woman's hair, right under "Be all that you can be." Over 95 percent of the people will not see this with their first look. Was this silhouette intentional? What do you think?

In figure 2-3 you probably saw a triangle that is whiter than the rest of the page. Note that no actual triangle is drawn there. Your eyes just imagined one being there based on the other figures. In addition, the whiteness of this mirage triangle is no brighter than the rest of the page.

If you saw everything there was to see in figure 2-4, you should have read the following in the two boxes.

A bird in the the hand is worth two in the ditch.

Not seeing the two *the*s is a case of not seeing what is actually there. In life we tend to do the same thing. We may see only one solution and not the many solutions that exist to our problems.

Classic Exercises with Nonclassic Solutions

Attempt the following exercises as a test of your creative abilities. You may have seen these exercises before. If you know a solution, then think up some others. Remember that creativity is going beyond what you already know to something new. Knowledge of the old is not creativity.

Exercise 2-3. The Old "Nine into Six" Trick

Change the roman numeral nine into a six by adding just one line.

I X

(A solution appears in Chapter Notes, page 19.)

Exercise 2-4. The "Classic" Nine-Circle Exercise

Part A

Connect all the nine circles below using *four* straight lines without lifting your pen or pencil from the surface. (If you can't solve this after ten minutes, see Chapter Notes, page 20, for a hint.)

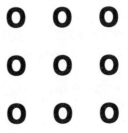

Part B

Now connect all the nine circles below using *three* straight lines, without lifting your pen or pencil from the surface.

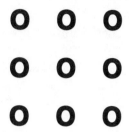

Part C

Now connect all the nine circles below using only *one* straight line, without lifting your pen or pencil from the surface.

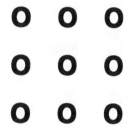

Chapter Notes

Exercise 2-3

The following solution is the standard one that is arrived at by overcoming the belief that a line can only be a straight line and the six has to be in roman numerals.

S I X

Many seminar presenters and motivational speakers use this exercise to emphasize creativity. However, they aren't very creative themselves, since they use the standard solution that they have seen elsewhere. They aren't being creative; they are just sharing knowledge acquired from someone else.

If seminar presenters using this exercise would have tried to be creative, they may have discovered there are at least seven more solutions to this exercise. See how many you can get. (Another solution appears in the Appendix, page 178.)

Exercise 2-4. Part A

You won't solve this exercise if you haven't told the truth about the problem. Recall that the first stage of creativity is identifying the problem. If you placed an imaginary barrier around the nine circles, note that none exists. Until you start extending the straight lines outside the imaginary barrier, you may not solve the problem. (See Appendix, page 178, for a solution.)

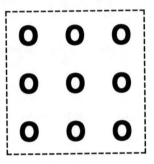

Exercise 2-4. Parts B and C

See Appendix, page 179, for solutions.

Do Be Do Be Do

You Can Be More Creative than Einstein or Picasso

While you are engaged in your journey through life, your creativity will be your resource for overcoming barriers such as society's norms, inadequate finances, objections of relatives, lack of skills, or limited time because of your children's needs. Creativity is the ultimate gift available to individuals dealing with the challenge of living happily. If anything will lead you out of boredom or a predicament, your imagination will. Highly creative individuals find that their most significant accomplishments occur when they are alone. New insights and discoveries usually don't involve the assistance of another person.

> Every child is an artist. The problem is how to remain an artist once he grows up.
>
> — *Pablo Picasso*

"But I'm not creative," you say. Nonsense! You were born creative, as was every human being. You have to rediscover your creativity and start using it to your advantage. So there you go! You have long suspected that you are a latent genius, but you haven't had the courage to share your suspicions with anyone. Now you can.

You can use your imagination to enhance your life in many ways. If you are a single parent, being more creative will help you manage your personal affairs, establish support networks, make ends meet on a low income, care for your children, and work at a full-time job (or two part-time ones) to support your household. Establishing a satisfying lifestyle, despite many obstacles, will prove you are much more creative than Einstein, Picasso, van Gogh, and Renoir ever were.

Dispelling Your Romantic Notions about Creativity

If you still aren't convinced that you are a creative genius, forget whatever romantic notions you have about creativity. Creativity isn't a gift from God given only to certain artists and musicians. Creativity also isn't dependent upon a lot of suffering, nor is it associated with a touch of madness. Some people think that one or more of the following factors are essential for anyone to be creative:

- Having rare artistic talent
- Having had parents who encouraged creativity
- Having an education in the fine arts
- Being right rather than left brained
- Having a high IQ
- Early independence as a child

I was fired from my last job for being too creative. I tried to design an off switch for a perpetual motion machine.

Creativity is often thought to be a matter of special skill, ability, knowledge, or effort. In fact, not one of the above factors is essential for creative success. If you take a hard look at creative people, they are simply "being" creative. They are expressing excellence and creativity, because they made the choice. Creative people don't believe they need exceptional talent to be creative.

To be is to do.
— *Camus*

To do is to be.
— *Sartre*

Do be do be do.
— *Frank Sinatra*

Many people believe that the sequence from *have* to *do* to *be* represents the road to creativity. Their belief is that a person must first *have* what creative people have: inherited intelligence, artistic talent, right-brain tilt, and a host of other things. Then the person will *do* what creative people do. Finally, the person will *be* creative. This belief is false. There is no truth to the belief that creative people have a special talent that enables them to be creative, and noncreative people don't have this talent. Researchers have confirmed that noncreative people have all the talent necessary to be creative.

I meet many people who want to be writers. More than "being" a writer, which takes effort and commitment, most of these people want all the trappings that accompany being a well-known writer. They want to have a best-selling book or two with their names on them and have the fame and fortune that Danielle Steele and John Grisham have. People also aspire to being writers because they want to do the things well-known writers do, such as participate at writers' conferences and appear on radio and television talk shows.

Being a writer doesn't happen after first having a best-selling book and appearing on talk shows to promote it. Aspiring writers can't ever do what writers do and have what writers have, unless they first choose to *be* writers. Being a writer doesn't happen after the doing and having. Being a writer first requires making the choice to *be* a writer, which leads to doing and having what writers do and have.

Reversing the above-stated sequence better represents the road to creativity. The right order is from *be* to *do* to *have*. First, we must choose to *be* creative. Then, we will *do* the things that creative people do. What will follow naturally is we will *have* the things that creative people have. The *have* things for a writer include accomplishment, satisfaction, and happiness experienced from attempting and completing a challenging project.

Creativity Principle:

Choose to Be Creative

This concept isn't something new. Taoism extols the importance of *being*. Classic Chinese Taoist philosophy was first documented by Lao-tzu some 2,500 years ago in his book *Tao-te-ching*. Lao-tzu emphasizes that to be truly alive, you must first *be*. Once you have mastered the art of *being*, then *doing* and *having* will flow naturally. *Being* is an active state — a creative process that helps you change and grow as a person. So, *be* creative or else!

Are You Too Intellectual to Be Creative?

Seymour Epstein, a psychologist at the University of Massachusetts, has found that constructive thinking is crucial for life success. Constructive thinking has almost nothing to do with our IQ. Constructive thinking involves taking action about a situation rather than complaining about it. Also, constructive thinkers don't take things personally and don't fret about what others think of them. Constructive thinking determines a great range of life's successes, from salaries and promotions, to happiness with friendships, to physical and emotional health.

> There are some things only intellectuals are crazy enough to believe.
> — *George Orwell*

Epstein found that many academically bright people do not think constructively. They have self-destructive habits of mind. They hold back from new challenges because they lack the necessary emotional smarts. Emotional intelligence was found by Epstein to be more important than academic intelligence. Epstein's findings shouldn't surprise many of us. We are already aware that many people with Ph.Ds are not very creative and some of the most creative people around don't even know what a Ph.D. is.

In certain ways, creative thinking is nothing more than common sense. It is the ability to question things and then take action accordingly. A doctorate degree or high intelligence level can't take the place of real-life experience combined with the power of imagination. Harry Gale took a little time to find this out. In early 1995, Gale was ousted from his position as executive director of MENSA in Britain. MENSA is an organization for people who have proven to have IQs representing something like the top 2 percent of the population. Apparently, Harry Gale finally saw the light as soon as he was sent down the road by this elitist organization. He set up a rival organization called Psicorp, which recruits members from all walks of life. In an interview with the *Sunday Times of London*, Gale stated, "Common sense is quite often more important than intelligence."

> There is nothing so irritating as somebody with less intelligence and more sense than we have.
> — *Don Herold*

Why don't more people choose to be constructive thinkers? My personal theory is that it is because becoming a constructive thinker takes effort and change. Most people resist anything that requires effort or change. Given the choice of doing something that is easy or something that is difficult, most people will opt for the easy. Why? Short-term comfort appeals to most people.

The choice of comfort is a paradox. Choosing to avoid the difficult is more comfortable in the short term; however, in the long term it results in discomfort. Most of us need to have tackled and conquered challenging tasks before we experience a sense of accomplishment and satisfaction.

So Much for the Easy Life

One of the biggest reasons for people being uncreative is their reluctance to take risks. People take the no-risk route because it is the most comfortable. All of us have the tendency to seek comfort at some time or other. In fact, most of us take the comfortable way all the time. The problem with choosing the comfortable way is in the long run it turns out to be very uncomfortable. This is best explained by what I call the "Easy Rule of Life." Figure 3-1 illustrates this rule. When we choose the easy and comfortable route, life turns out to be difficult. Ninety percent of people choose this route because short-term comfort is the more appealing than difficulty.

Figure 3-1. The Easy Rule of Life

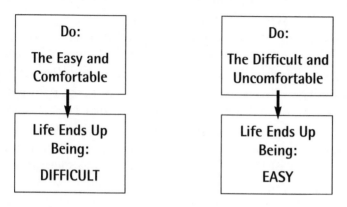

The other option is to take the difficult and uncomfortable route. When we choose the difficult and uncomfortable route, life is easy. Ten percent of people take this route because they know they must experience short-term discomfort for long-term gains. They also know there is much less competition than on the other route. The Easy Rule of Life influences every area of life, including work, financial gain, friendship, love, health, leisure, and overall satisfaction.

Ashleigh Brilliant said, "I have abandoned the search for truth, and am now looking for a good fantasy." I trust that you haven't done the same. It is important that you aren't carried away by illusions about life. The bad news is that this book can't lead you to that promised land, about halfway between Nirvana and Shangri-la. If you were expecting that life could be one big party, I am sorry to have disappointed you.

> All things are difficult before they are easy.
> — *Unknown Wise Person*

After the bad news, I have some really good news. The good news is that all individuals — including you — can live in a paradise. To have a happy and successful life, you must utilize the Easy Rule of Life and follow the principles in this book.

Being a happy individual is dependent upon making up your mind to make the best of your situation. This will take some effort; it will also be uncomfortable at times. Taking the easy and comfortable way — sitting at home and blaming the world — will put you on a dead-end street. Long-term satisfaction can only be attained by undertaking the challenging activities that are at times somewhat difficult. A price has to paid in terms of time and effort. If you are no longer a juvenile, you should have learned by now that nothing of major consequence in life comes easily. You must pay the price of a little discomfort for anything that adds to your long-term happiness.

> If you want the rainbow, you gotta put up with the rain.
> — *Dolly Parton*

You may now be thinking the same thing that a woman at a recent seminar said to me, "Zelinski, who are you? Some kind of sadist? You are advocating nothing but a whole lot of suffering in this world for me." On the contrary, I am not advocating anything of that nature. Keep in mind that I don't work more than four or five hours a day. Also, as much as possible, I avoid working in any month that doesn't have an *r* in it. This is not suffering. I enjoy life. It is more than just something to do. I am a proponent of a little discomfort now and then, which all adds up to a big payoff of satisfaction and happiness in the long term.

Have you ever experienced an incredible high after you accomplished something that you initially didn't think you could accomplish or something that everyone else said couldn't be done? For example, if you quit smoking, I bet what you accomplished wasn't easy. And yet, by undertaking the difficult and uncomfortable, you achieved a great deal of satisfaction from your accomplishment. This was the Easy Rule of Life in action.

> The difficult we do immediately. The impossible takes a little longer.
> — *Slogan of the U.S. Army Service Forces*

Being happy takes commitment and effort. You must take responsibility for your life if you want to create a paradise where you are happy and fulfilled. You have already taken some responsibility by reading at least a portion of this book. Richard Bach, in his book *Illusions*, wrote, "Every person, all the events of your life are there because you have drawn them there." Let's say that at some level you took responsibility and utilized your tremendous mental powers to create me writing this book for you. Yes, if it wasn't for you, at the time of my writing this book I could have been in Vancouver cycling around Stanley Park, wining and dining at Chianti's Restaurant, and having coffee at the Bread Garden or Starbucks while waiting for my soulmate to show up. However, I trust that you will allow me to take the next two or three summers off, so I can do these and a host of other enjoyable things before you use your mental powers to create me writing another book for you.

It's Publish and Creatively Promote or Perish

Many people have written or phoned me due to the success of my self-published book, *The Joy of Not Working*. Most of these people think I have found the easy way to make a book a best-seller; however, the Easy Rule of Life applies here.

The letter I send to all people who contact me about publishing is presented below. The main point is that it takes creativity and effort to establish a best-seller. Creativity and effort are required not only in writing a book; but also for promoting the book. This requires doing the difficult and uncomfortable instead of the easy and comfortable.

> If people knew what they had to do to be successful, most people wouldn't.
>
> — *Lord Thomson of Fleet*

Dear Aspiring Author:

So you want to be a successful writer with a best-seller or two. Contrary to what most people believe, I don't have a secret formula for making a book a best-seller. However, I can offer some basic advice which I consider extremely important for creating a best-seller.

First and foremost, if you want to write a best-selling book because you think it is an easy way to fame and fortune, do yourself a favor by pursuing something else immediately. Writing a book and making it a best-seller is much more difficult than getting an undergraduate university degree, going on to a master's degree, topping it up with a doctorate degree, and finally landing a job, as hard as it is to land a job today. Don't believe me? Just remember that there are a lot more people with doctorate degrees than there are people who have written best-selling books. Besides, if it was so easy to create a best-selling book, practically everyone would be doing it. If you haven't noticed, about 99 percent of the people always take the easy way out in life. That's why they will never have a best-selling book.

Here is the second important test: How good are you at celebrating failure and being motivated by criticism and rejection? Creating a best-seller will require that you accept and celebrate failure. Writing and promoting a book to make it a best-seller will require that you are not only able to cope with, but more important, be motivated by criticism and rejection. For example, when *The Joy of Not Working* made the *Globe and Mail*'s list of books that definitely would *not* be reviewed by their book section, I was motivated to show them that my book would outsell 99 percent of all the books they review.

If you have passed the above two tests with flying colors, then there may be hope for you. Now go out and buy and read all the books you can find on writing, publishing, and promotion. (Note, I said *buy* these books, not borrow them. If you won't buy someone else's books, why should you expect anyone to buy yours?)

Next, what are you going to write about? The most important principle here is to select a topic for which there is a market. *You have to first ask yourself: "Who is going to want to buy my book?" Then you better have a damn good answer.*

Just because you think people should be reading books in your chosen topic doesn't mean there will be a market for your book. Don't fall into the trap like so many people (including major publishers) who go on the basis of what they think other people should be reading. Your opinion of what is important, or what ought to be important to people, is totally irrelevant. The people who buy books are the ones who will decide what is important to them. This is the way it should be; it's their money.

Once you have completed a book and had it published, you are about 5 percent of the way there to making it a best-seller. Whether the book is self-published or published by a major publisher, you must promote your product. You can have the best product in the world, but if you can't market it, you may as well have the worst product. The best promotion for a book is not done by publishers, distributors, or bookstores; the best promotion is done by the author. *In the academic world, it's publish or perish. In the real world, it's publish and* promote *or perish.*

Writing a good book takes creativity; effective promotion takes ten times as much creativity. Five years after I wrote *The Joy of Not Working* I am still promoting the book with the same level of effort and creativity as when the book was first released. I will be doing this for at least another two years.

> Opportunities are usually disguised as hard work, so most people don't recognize them.
>
> — *Ann Landers*

Another very important point: You have to start by doing. All the knowledge in the world isn't going to help you if you don't do something with it.

Finally, I could wish you luck but I won't — luck isn't what will get you there. Your own motivation, determination, and creativity will get you there.

Sincerely,

Ernie J. Zelinski

Don't Pay the Price; Enjoy the Price

Let me warn you that the Easy Rule of Life is something like the law of gravity. Mess around with the law of gravity by walking off the top of a building and see what happens to you. It knocks you on your butt. The same thing applies with the Easy Rule of Life. Mess around with it by taking the easy way, and you wind up on your butt as well. It seems to work all the time. Note, this is the way life is. Please don't blame me for the way it is; I didn't set it up this way. I just observed that life is this way, and we have to make the best of it.

> If people knew how hard I worked to get my mastery, it wouldn't seem so wonderful at all.
>
> — *Michelangelo*

The biggest obstacle to success is the discomfort in doing the necessary things we must do to attain success. As human beings we gravitate towards less pain and more pleasure. The majority of us opt for the easy way because we are seeking comfort at all costs. Roads on which there is a lot of traffic tend to have a lot of ruts.

Choosing the easy way in life ensures we wind up in one or more of these ruts. And the only difference between a rut and a grave are the dimensions. In the rut you get to join the "living dead," and in the grave you get to join the "dead dead."

Everything in life has a price. Most people take the course of inaction because at the time it seems the easiest. In the end they cheat themselves out of the big payoffs. Take my advice and don't be one of the majority who choose comfort at the expense of accomplishment and satisfaction. The real prizes in life come to us when we are willing to do things somewhat difficult and uncomfortable. Choosing to be creative is one of them.

There is a price to pay in making the effort to be creative, just as there is in anything worthwhile in life. But rather than looking at the price we have to pay, let us look at the many prices we get to enjoy. Prices to enjoy include higher self-esteem, greater satisfaction, increased happiness, and more peace of mind. Indeed, the price is to be more enjoyed than paid. Creativity involves doing the difficult and uncomfortable; the payoff is that it is much more rewarding and satisfying than doing the easy and comfortable.

CHAPTER 4

101 Ways to Skin a Cat or Do Just About Anything

Getting the "Right Answer" May Put You on the Wrong Track

Let us begin this chapter with the following two exercises.

Exercise 4-1

Big Rock Brewery of Calgary couldn't afford the traditional beer marketing promotions large breweries use when it was about to introduce its beer products to the extremely competitive markets in Canada and the United States. Big Rock has been able to introduce its products with great success and have sales grow substantially while Canada's big breweries have been consolidating and battling over a shrinking market.

What is the answer? . . . [silence in reply]. In that case, what is the question?

— *Gertrude Stein*

How would you have handled the problem of little money for advertising to launch new beer products in a competitive and shrinking market?

Exercise 4–2. The Unique Pair of Scissors

Which pair of scissors is different from all the others?

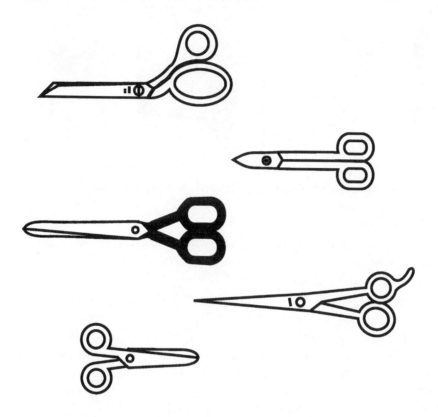

A North American and a European were discussing the joys of life when the European stated that he knew 100 different ways to make love. The North American was highly impressed with this. He told the European he knew only one. The European asked him which one it was. The North American described the most natural and conventional way there is. The European then replied to the North American, "That is amazing! I never thought of that! Thanks. Now I know 101."

Are you like the North American or the European when solving problems? Do you come up with only one solution or many? We have all heard the saying "There is more than one way to skin a cat." Yet how many of us would look for several ways to skin a cat if we had to skin one.

> I once made love for an hour and fifteen minutes but it was the night the clocks are set ahead.
>
> — *Garry Shandling*

Most of us are apt to look for one way to do most tasks. If this single way does not work well, we still stick with it and find someone or something to blame for the situation being unworkable. We do not look

CALVIN AND HOBBES

for new ways. Another way may be quicker, more efficient, or less costly. Last, but not least, it could plainly be more fun. Ask the European if you ever run into him.

Let us return to exercise 4-1. Were you looking for the one right way of overcoming the problem? Did you stop after one solution or did you come up with many alternatives?

How Big Rock Brewery handled it is not the only way (see Chapter Notes, page 36). Many solutions are available. The management of Big Rock could have borrowed money for advertising. They could have sold shares in the company to generate additional money for advertising. Partnership with an established brewery was an option, as was generating publicity through some offbeat activity. The list of options is endless.

> There are nine ways of poaching eggs, and each of them is worse than the other.
>
> — Robert Lynd

Exercise 4-2 gives more evidence of how we approach problems. Did you overlook the obvious like nine out of ten people do on this exercise? Ninety percent of participants in my seminars end up choosing one of the five pairs of scissors. Everyone is right to a certain degree, but most participants miss the main point. That is because the answer is, "all the pairs of scissors are different from all the others."

This exercise demonstrates how well the school systems have taught us to automatically look for the one right answer or one way of doing things. In doing so, we become very structured in our responses. We tend to stop looking for more "right answers." When the only "right" answer we come up with is a "dud," we are lost.

One of the most important creativity principles is there are two or more solutions to all problems. Two exceptions to the rule exist. One is in mathematics. Half of thirteen has only one answer. (Note we will see in chapter 9 that even this problem may have more than one solution.) In mathematics most problems have one solution. The only other time there are less than two solutions is when we are dead. Then there are no solutions. Generally speaking, life's problems have two or more solutions.

Possibility in life's situations extends beyond the available and obvious. What do we have to do to create many new solutions? It is essential we first let go of the old and go to a state of nothing. Yes, we must start from nothing. Opportunity is literally created from a state of nothingness. When we let go of old solutions and old ways of thinking, we have a clear slate from which we can create.

Break It Before Someone Else Breaks It

Looking for options requires effort. It is easier to look for alternatives when we are dissatisfied with the alternatives we have at hand. However, we should look for more solutions even when the ones we already have appeal to us. Care should be taken in not necessarily limiting ourselves to the first few alternatives we generate. Disciplining ourselves to keep looking for other alternatives, even when we are satisfied with some of those already generated, is a good practice.

Creativity Principle:

Look for Many Solutions

Better solutions and alternatives should be strived for even when things appear to be going well. Attempts at inventing better alternatives when a good one is already available have three main benefits:

- This provides some insurance that a better alternative has not been overlooked. The successful alternative in use may not be the best available.

- Most, if not all, good things come to an end. People who generate alternatives when things are going well have other solutions to fall back on when the present solution is no longer effective due to changing circumstances.

- People continually involved in the selection of alternatives, whether needed or not, will keep their creative talents in practice for when they are needed.

The old adage "If it works, don't fix it" is questionable in this day and age. Even if it is working fine, it probably won't for very long in a competitive and rapidly changing business world. Having the ability to generate many solutions allows us to react much more effectively when it does break down.

Robert J. Kriegel and Louis Patler, in their book *If It Ain't Broke . . . BREAK IT!* go so far as to say break it before it breaks on its own, or before someone else breaks it. Following Kriegel's and Patler's philosophy will help you be innovative and put you way ahead of 99 percent of the people who will wait for it to break down before they attempt to fix it.

> Doing the same thing over and over, expecting different results is the definition of crazy.
> — *Unknown Wise Person*

Exercises to Motivate You to Look and Look and Look

Exercise 4-3. Triangles Galore (If You Look)

The diagram below is a perspective builder. You simply have to count the number of triangles in the diagram. (See Chapter Notes, page 36, when you are finished.)

> If it works, it's obsolete.
> — *Marshall McLuhan*

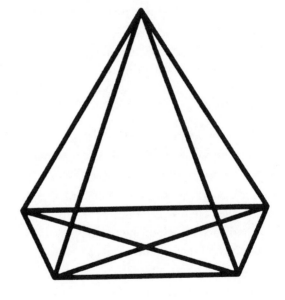

Exercise 4-4. Playing with Matches

In preparation for the next chapter, let us try another type of exercise. Assume the following two equations are made with matchsticks. Each line in the characters is one matchstick. Both equations are wrong as they stand. Can you, by moving just one matchstick in each equation, make the equations correct? Start with (a) and only proceed to (b) when you have completed (a). (See Chapter Notes, page 36, when you are finished.)

(a)

(b)

Exercise 4-5. A Quota of New Ideas

Do this exercise regularly. Set a goal to generate at least three new ideas daily for your most important project or problem.

I don't give a damn for
any man who can spell
a word only one way.
— *Mark Twain*

Chapter Notes

Exercise 4-1

Big Rock Brewery first focused on the huge Californian market by introducing products with unorthodox beer names such as Buzzard Breath, Warthog Ale, and Albino Rhino. At the time of my writing this book, Big Rock has introduced a new product called Grasshopper Ale. A large part of Big Rock's success has been their names. As Big Rock's U.S. distributor, Bill Gibbs of Claymore Beverage says, "Warthog Ale just lunges off the shelf at you."

> In the republic of mediocrity, genius is dangerous.
>
> — *Robert Ingersoll*

Big Rock has established credibility at the high end of the market in the trendy professional restaurants by targeting promotions at theater groups, folk festivals, ballet, and opera instead of the traditional groups that the large breweries go after. Big Rock's beers sell at a premium of $15.00 a case in comparison to the $10.00 to $12.00 a case the large breweries charge for their products.

Exercise 4-2

They are all different from all the others.

Exercise 4-3

Most people see fewer than twenty-five triangles in this figure. There are thirty-five triangles if you really look.

Exercise 4-4

Did you proceed to *b* after getting only one solution for *a*? These two exercises are a test for how well you mastered the principle of looking for more than one solution. Notice how easy it is to stop after only one solution. If you didn't get at least three solutions to both exercises, you are in the majority. Now go back and try again. (Exercise *a* has at least thirty solutions. If you attend one of my creativity seminars, I will show you several blockbuster solutions to exercise *a* that only one in one thousand people will see. Exercise *b* has over ten solutions. See Appendix, page 179, for some of mine.)

CHAPTER 5

A Great Memory for Forgetting

Is Your Photographic Memory Out of Film?

How good is your memory? The intent of this chapter is to underscore the importance of writing our ideas down. We have a tendency to avoid writing down ideas, thinking that we will remember them later. This is a mistake. We aren't as good at remembering things as we think we are.

The following exercises will demonstrate this.

Exercise 5-1. I'm Too Old to Remember That!

Draw the dial of a nondigital telephone, that is, one having a rotary dial rather than a push-button one. Place all the finger holes in the right position on the dial and then record the position of all the numbers and letters. This is something that you have seen many times, so it won't be a problem to remember. Right!

If you think you are too young (or too old) to remember the rotary telephone, try this exercise with a modern push-button telephone. Try to remember the numbers and the corresponding letters that go on the different keys.

I always have trouble remembering three things: faces, names, and . . . I don't remember what the third thing is.

— *Fred Allen*

Now refer to the back of this chapter (page 44) to see how well you did on the above exercise. If you didn't get the layout of the rotary telephone (or the push-button one) completely, you are definitely in the majority. Most of us have a hard time remembering what either dial precisely looks like. Let us try another exercise.

Exercise 5-2. Remembering a Robbery

Recall the cartoon with the two robbers in chapter 2. Assume you witnessed that attempted robbery and have been asked by the police department to identify the two robbers. Without looking back at the cartoon on page 12, try to pick the two men who were attempting the creativity robbery out of the twelve in the following figure.

By now some of you are probably getting worried about your memories being shot because of your age. Not so. Look at children. Ask a schoolteacher whether children forget things at school. The schoolteacher will list things like coats, lunch boxes, gloves, books, combs, pencils, pens, and much more. Children don't forget because of their age; neither do we. We forget because of the many distractions we have in our lives.

I never forget a face, but in your case I'll make an exception.

— Groucho Marx

"Almost anything you do today will be forgotten in just a few weeks," states John McCrone in the March 1994 issue of New Scientist. "The ability to retrieve a memory decays exponentially, and after only a month more than 85 percent of our experiences will have slipped beyond reach, unless boosted by artificial aids such as diaries and photographs."

Not remembering the dial on the telephone or the two faces in a picture is not a serious thing. However, forgetting good ideas for our problems may cost us wonderful or blockbuster solutions. Ideas are easily forgotten. Exercise 5-3 may give more evidence of this.

Exercise 5-3. Thinking About Your Past Thinking

Write down the thoughts that you were thinking at exactly this time of the day one week ago. In addition, write down all the good ideas you had about solutions to your problems, someone else's problems, or to society's problems in the last week.

How did you do? If you could not remember much about what you were thinking one week ago, how do you know if you have forgotten one or more blockbuster ideas that you had right at that time? How about all the ideas during the week since then? Possibly you had some useful ideas that you didn't write down and have since forgotten.

To deal with the tendency of their employees to forget good ideas, some organizations have put their company writing pads and pens in locker rooms in company gyms. These are for recording ideas that the employees may think of while exercising or in the shower. There is a good reason for this practice. Many good ideas are generated when people exercise. Good ideas tend to come from the altered state of mind that exercise produces. The companies want to be sure that the ideas are recorded immediately and not lost with time.

Creativity Principle:

Write Down All Your Ideas

If our ideas are not recorded immediately, we risk not recalling them later. What causes us to forget at a later time is our changed state of mind. Our minds are overworked trying to remember the many things for everyday living. When we become totally engrossed in something related to other work assignments or to our personal lives, the last thing on our minds is the good idea we had one or two days ago while in the shower.

To totally convince yourself about the importance of recording your ideas and solutions, do one last exercise. When you are working on a special project, write down all the ideas that you get and put them in a file. Be extremely disciplined about this. Don't forget to record anything. Do this for two weeks and during these two weeks do not review the contents of the file. At the end of the two weeks try to remember everything that went in the file. Then look in the file. You may be surprised at the number of ideas that you have forgotten.

Growing an Idea Tree

You can write your ideas, answers, and solutions for a special problem or project in many different forms. You can make a list, use sentences, or write an essay. These all have their places; however, there is a better tool for recording ideas. This device is especially useful in the initial stages of solving a problem or working on a project.

I finally got it all together and then I forgot where I put it.

— Unknown Wise Person

The tool is an idea tree. This tool is also known as a mind map, spoke diagram, thought web, and clustering diagram.

The idea tree is simple but powerful. The surprising thing is that most of us were never shown how to use an idea tree when attending school. I first learned about it from a waiter in a restaurant.

Here is how an idea tree is created. Starting at the center of the page, the goal, theme, or purpose of the idea tree is recorded. For example, if you are generating an idea tree for the ways in which you want to market a new management book, you can write this down as in figure 5-1.

From the central theme, branches or lines are drawn toward the boundary of the page. Print any ideas on these branches that relate to the problem or project. Primary ideas are recorded on separate branches near the center of the page. Secondary branches are then drawn extending from the primary ones. This is where the secondary ideas that relate to the main ones are recorded. More branches off the secondary ones can be drawn to record a third level of ideas.

Figure 5-1. An Idea Tree for Generating Ideas on How to Market a New Book on Management

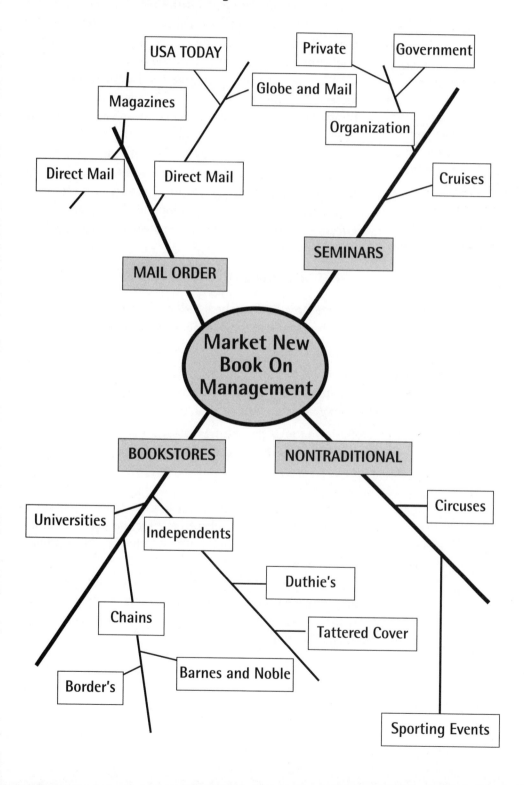

One primary idea for marketing a new management book is to market the book in bookstores. The word *Bookstores* is recorded as one of the primary ideas on the idea tree in figure 5-1. Then secondary ideas are generated to enlarge on the types of bookstores. Chains, university, and independent bookstores are listed on the second level of ideas. A third level of ideas is used to enlarge on the chain bookstores. Here we include the Barnes and Noble and the Border's bookstore chains. More levels of ideas can be added if needed.

This tool is a powerful way of generating a lot of ideas quickly. Although the idea tree is meant to be a tool for individual brainstorming, it can be adapted for group use without any problems. Let us look at the reasons for the effectiveness of the idea tree as an idea-generating tool.

> A man would do well to carry a pencil in his pocket, and write down the thoughts of the moment. Those that come unsought for are commonly the most valuable, and should be secured, because they seldom return.
> — *Francis Bacon*

Advantages of the Idea Tree

- It is compact. Many ideas can be listed on one page. If needed, the idea tree can be expanded to additional pages.
- Ideas are put in categories. This makes it easier to group ideas.
- The creator of an idea tree can hitchhike on his or her own ideas to generate many other ideas. This works in much the same way as hitchhiking in group brainstorming.
- It is a long-term tool. After setting it aside for a day or a week, the person using the tree can come back and generate a batch of fresh ideas.

Idea trees are not only used for the right-brain activity of rapid idea generation. Another way to use an idea tree is for the purpose of self-discovery, by way of clustering thoughts about such things as what your relationship is with money.

Left-brain activities such as planning and organizing also lend themselves to being performed on idea trees. Short-range plans, long-range plans, diaries, speech plans, goals, and records of lecture notes can be created with this useful tool.

Figure 5-2. An Idea Tree (Using Visuals) for Generating Ideas on What to Do on a Long Weekend

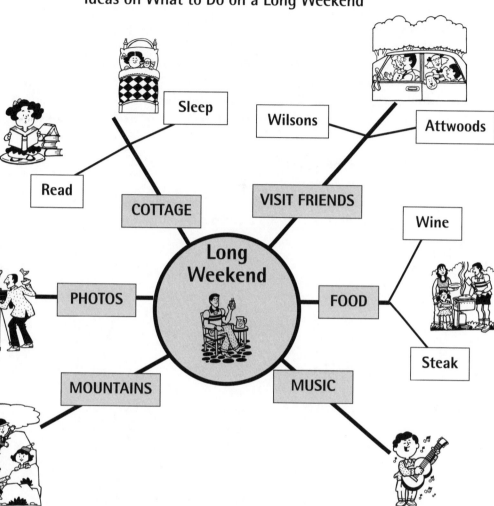

Figure 5-2 shows a more advanced idea tree that uses images. Images are used to enhance creativity and memory. Color can be used along with images to add to the effect of the idea tree.

Idea trees require more work than do ordinary lists; however, the extra work is well worth it. Remember the Easy Rule of Life from chapter 3. By putting in the extra work in constructing this more difficult and challenging tool, you will be a lot better off in the long run than you are with ordinary lists or by not using any tool at all.

Who of major consequence has used idea trees? Only such people as Albert Einstein, Leonardo da Vinci, Thomas Jefferson, John F. Kennedy, and Thomas Edison. I think this is a good group with which to be associated.

Chapter Notes

Exercise 5-1

Not one in a thousand people in my seminars will get this exactly. Note that there are some things you did not notice about the rotary telephone dial even though you have seen it many times. These are things that were staring you in the face but you never saw. Why? You never put in the effort to look. Similarly, many solutions to our problems stare us in our faces. We do not see these solutions because of our lack of effort in looking.

a) The *1* has no letters beside it.

b) The *Q* and *Z* are not used.

c) The letters go clockwise in ABC, DEF, GHI, and JKL. The letters go counterclockwise in all the other sets of three letters.

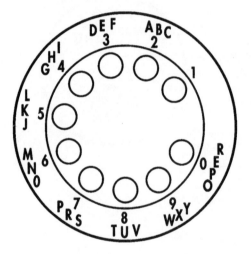

As you can see, the layout of the push-button telephone is not much easier to remember.

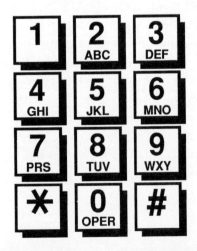

CHAPTER 6

The Advantages of Drinking On the Job

Cycle Designed by a Psycho?

The best way to emphasize the point of this chapter is to start with the following exercise.

Exercise 6-1

You have been hired by a major bicycle manufacturer as a consultant. Your job is to evaluate the merits of the bicycle designs that designers submit to the manufacturer. The manufacturer has asked for a new design for a tandem bicycle.

One of the designs that the manufacturer received is my design shown above. Although my undergraduate degree is in electrical engineering, I decided I could design something mechanical. (I know you are impressed.)

Write down the main points about my design for a new tandem bicycle that you will put in your report to the manufacturer. Be honest in your evaluation and don't be afraid of hurting my ego.

Let's look at my bicycle design in exercise 6-1. What points did you choose for your report? Are your points all negative? If they are, you haven't fully explored my design. Unless you put down some positive points, some negative points, and some in between, you have jumped to conclusions without due consideration to my "wonderful" design. Your voice of judgment (VOJ) has stepped in too soon.

Good judgment comes from experience; and experience, well, that comes from bad judgment.

— *Unknown Wise Person*

You should have considered such positive points as the rear wheel can be used as a spare for the front in case the front tire goes flat. How about a more comfortable ride because of two back wheels? This bicycle could also have an advantage over conventional ones for carrying heavy loads. It is great for overweight people. People may want to buy it as a status symbol, since it is a new and different design.

On the negative side, the bicycle may be awkward to ride. The back wheel may be excess baggage. It looks ridiculous. There is no second seat for an extra person.

There are many points to be made for both the positive and negative aspects of this design. To fully explore the merits of this design, we should write down and consider all these points. Then we can make a decision based on a comprehensive evaluation of this new idea for a bicycle.

Exercise 6-2

You are the owner of a medium-size advertising agency. To remain competitive, your company is looking for new markets and new opportunities. Two weeks ago you introduced a suggestion box to encourage new ideas from the employees. As you are going through the latest ideas in the suggestion box, a rather odd suggestion appears. The suggestion says, "Our new promotional flyers belong in washroom stalls."

What should you do with this suggestion?

1. Assume it is a practical joke, chuckle and disregard it.

2. Assume the idea is serious but the originator is demented.

3. Assume it means that the new flyers are ineffective.

4. Assume the idea is serious and has some merits.

Don't Nuke Your Ideas with VOJ

Your voice of judgment (VOJ) may have affected the answer that you chose in Exercise 6-2. Did you choose to ignore or eliminate the washroom stalls as a viable advertising medium? If you did, think again. An entrepreneur in the United States is generating millions of dollars of revenue annually by selling advertising space in washrooms of businesses and airplanes. The idea was spawned when he left sales brochures in washrooms and he started getting great responses. One of the biggest advantages is that the audience is more captive with this form of advertising. If you did not give this advertising medium any consideration, it is because you were the victim of your voice of judgment. This prevented you from fully exploring this idea.

Creativity Principle:

Fully Analyze Your Ideas

We are all victims of our voices of judgment. This is the rational part of us that can jump in and destroy an idea before it has a chance to blossom. Many good ideas are not given full consideration. We tend to find something negative about these ideas and promptly discard them. The reverse is also true. We may promptly accept an idea without looking at all the negatives.

Some Great "Wacky" Ideas Saved from VOJ

Many successful ideas have been spared execution by others' VOJ because the originators of these ideas had the presence of mind to fully explore them for their value. Most people in our society would not have given these ideas any consideration at all. Yet due to the ideas' success, they are taken for granted as being the norm today.

- By accidently preparing grain too long, the Kellogg brothers in the late 1800s wound up with a new product that they decided to introduce as a cold cereal. Until then cereal was always eaten hot. Most marketing experts predicted imminent failure for this product, which they labeled "Horse Food." The Kelloggs called this product, still popular today, "cornflakes."

- Over ten years ago, Bill Comrie, along with two partners, took over his father's small furniture sales store in Edmonton, Alberta. Today Bill Comrie owns the Brick Furniture stores that compose one of the biggest furniture chains in North America. One of Comrie's first marketing tools was the "Midnight Madness Sale." The first one he proposed was questioned by his two partners. They claimed no one would show up. Well, show up they did. The furniture store did more business during that one night than Bill Comrie's father had done in the previous year in the store. The Midnight Madness Sale was used with great success in the early days of the Brick's phenomenal growth.

- On the night that the idea for the Pet Rock was conceived, several people laughed and joked about this great pet that everyone would want. Of course, this was a ridiculous idea to everyone except for Gary Dahl. He went home and could not sleep because of the idea's promise. It was then that he overcame his VOJ and decided to market a book giving instructions on how to care for a Pet Rock. Its success is history.

Darn it, why didn't I think of this ingenious bicycle?

- Even Post-it Notes almost got nuked by VOJ. The idea of Post-it Notes originated in 1974 with Art Fry, a 3M employee who sang in a choir. He used bits of paper to mark the hymns, but the papers kept falling out of his books. He went into the office one day and made some papers with adhesive backing. These worked well. When 3M decided to look into marketing a commercial variation of these notes, distributors thought they were silly. Initial market surveys offered little promise. The 3M company did not allow others' voices of judgment to interfere with the development of this product. A mailing of samples to secretaries of large companies showed a favorable interest. Introduced in 1980, Post-it Notes now bring in over $400 million in annual revenue to the 3M corporation.

Don't Bank on Your Banker or Suggestion Programs

If you have had bank managers discard your ideas as wacky, you are not the only one who has learned that you can't bank on your banker liking your ideas. A banker once told Alexander Graham Bell to get out of his bank with "that ridiculous toy." This so-called "ridiculous toy" was one of Bell's first models of the telephone.

Getting your banker to think positively about your product may be quite a challenge. In one of my seminar presentations to a banking institution, I used the tandem bicycle from exercise 6-1 to determine whether its bank managers fully explore ideas, that is, evaluate ideas on both positive and negative qualities. Out of about ten comments, there wasn't one positive one. Considering that the bicycle does have some positive attributes, I had to conclude that these bankers were trained to, above all, focus on the negatives. It is no wonder that many good business proposals will receive little financial support from most banks.

> When a true genius appears in the world, you may know him by this sign, that the dunces are all in confederacy against him.
>
> — *Jonathan Swift*

Incidentally, I also had the opportunity to do a seminar for members of an association who ran suggestion programs for their respective companies. These people didn't fare any better than the bankers; not one positive comment was made about the tandem bicycle. I was amazed that these people who ran suggestion programs didn't know how to fully analyze ideas properly.

Suggestion boxes offer some evidence of the power of people's VOJ. Some companies report that over 50 percent of their employees' ideas have merit. Toyota claims its Creative Idea Suggestion System has generated over 20 million ideas in forty years, with more than 90 percent of them accepted.

Other companies report that less than 5 percent of employees' suggestions have any value. Why the big difference? Surely more than 5 percent of ideas in any company are useful. In all likelihood, the managers of companies that use only a minute number of all ideas submitted are discarding a lot of good ideas. They don't fully explore them for all the positives. They focus on the negatives and discard ideas without any further consideration.

Attack of the VOJ Idea Killers

"It will never work. It's a dumb idea!" If you have had an idea that was different, chances are you were told it would never work by your colleagues, friends, or family. Practically any successful entrepreneur who has succeeded in developing a radically new service or product has heard this voice-of-judgment idea killer.

Here are just a few of the many VOJ idea killers used to attack an innovative person suggesting something new and different:

- Why hasn't someone else thought of this before?
- Someone else tried something similar and failed.
- It will take a lot of work.
- She has no experience in our industry.
- It will cost too much.
- Top management will never approve it.
- People will think we are crazy.

Treat All Your Ideas to Some PMI

The PMI method is a powerful thinking tool developed by Edward de Bono. It is powerful but simple. Everybody will think they use it all the time; however, a lot of people don't use it at all. In fact, highly intellectual people are more prone than others to ignore this method because of their confidence in their viewpoint as being the only right one.

The PMI method of thinking is a tool used over a period of a few minutes (two to five) to focus attention on the idea at hand. It is deliberate and is performed in a very disciplined manner to give a more complete exploration of the idea.

PMI is an abbreviation for the types of things that one should consider in the analysis of an idea or a solution to a problem. The letters stand for the following:

What a great bicycle! Sure beats having him ride me.

- *P* stands for Plus (positive points)
- *M* stands for Minus (negative points)
- *I* stands for Interesting (neutral points)

PMI as an Idea Analyzer

If we were to ask fifty people what they thought about the idea of the government giving everyone $5,000 to stimulate the economy, a majority may think it is a good idea. Then, if we asked these same people to reconsider using the PMI method of thinking, we would undoubtedly get some different results. The PMI analysis could look something like this:

PLUS	MINUS	INTERESTING
More spending will result. People will be happier. More jobs will be created. Children will leave home.	Our taxes will go up. Drug addicts will buy drugs and alcoholics will drink themselves silly. More resources will be used up. Inflation will increase. Children will leave home.	It will be interesting to see how much money is banked. It will be interesting to see what people will spend money on. It will be interesting to see if charitable donations increase.

Note the *interesting* component of the PMI technique has several uses. First, the comments that are neither favorable nor unfavorable can be placed here. Second, the thinker is encouraged to look outside the normal judgmental framework of good or bad. Last, this aspect can lead the thinker to look at another idea by hitchhiking on the one being considered.

When people force themselves to use the PMI method, they usually find that their feelings about the topic change from what they felt at the outset. The final decision can be somewhat of a surprise to themselves. PMI is most useful in those situations where we feel sure about our conclusion from the outset. That is when we need to use this form of analysis the most.

> The jean! The jean is the destructor. It is a dictator! It is destroying creativity! The jean must be stopped!
> — *Pierre Cardin*

Exercise 6-3. The Advantages (and Disadvantages) of Drinking on the Job

Assume you run a suggestion program for a large corporation and someone has submitted the following suggestion for increasing productivity:

We should allow employees to drink (alcoholic beverages) on the job.

Do a PMI analysis on this suggestion to ensure that you fully explore it for its merits. (See Appendix, page 180, for a sample analysis.)

PLUS	MINUS	INTERESTING

Most Organizations Say They Are Innovative — So What?

I drink only to make my friends seem more interesting.

— *Unknown Wise Person*

Let us look at why your innovative ideas and creativity will not find much support in many of today's organizations. This will happen despite the need for organizations to be highly innovative to survive and prosper in a competitive global economy. Here is an exercise to underscore the way many North American organizations function.

Exercise 6-4. Only Time Will Tell

Tom Beller, a manager of the marketing department in a large company, is faced with a major problem. The company is attempting to deal with the present business environment, which is highly competitive. It is not only constantly changing, but rapidly changing. Constant innovation is necessary to keep ahead of the major competitors.

The immediate problem is with one of the company's best employees, Trina Hamper. She is constantly late for work by about half an hour and shows no sign of improvement. In the manager's opinion, Trina is undoubtedly the department's most valuable employee in the areas of innovation and productivity. She is independent, energetic, and highly creative. The quality of her work is superior to anyone else's. Tom holds her in high esteem and has shown this by rapidly promoting her and giving her more raises than anyone in the company has ever received. In contrast, most of Trina's peers hold her in low esteem and tend to dislike her. So do some of the employees in senior management. She is constantly criticized. Her coming in late is one of several things she is criticized for.

Lately, other employees in the company have started coming in late. When confronted about this, they have replied that if Trina can get away with being late, so should they.

What should Tom Beller do to rectify this problem?

Today's most prominent management consultants state that successful companies of the 1990s and beyond will have to fit the following profile:

- Have well-trained, creative, and flexible employees
- Provide key employees opportunity for personal growth
- Differentiate their service
- Be quality conscious
- Be lean but extremely responsive
- Be highly innovative

> What luck for rulers that men do not think.
> — *Adolf Hitler*

The case study in exercise 6-4 represents a situation that, according to participants of my seminars and courses, occurs often in the real world of organizations. (See Chapter Notes, pages 63 through 65, for potential solutions.) The situation of a highly creative person not being supported has several implications.

Let us look at the qualities or traits highly creative people such as Trina display.

Traits of Highly Creative Employees

- Independent
- Persistent
- Highly motivated and very productive
- Risk takers
- Spontaneous and strong sense of humor
- Use intuition and emotions in decision making
- Have a good balance between work and play
- Have desire for privacy
- Can be renegades
- Prefer complex and asymmetrical tasks rather than the simple and symmetrical
- Have resistance to indoctrination
- Can be hard to get along with at times
- Will take stands on issues
- Relish disorder and ambiguity
- Question things, especially the status quo
- Cause problems and don't care

The most important thing to recognize in the case represented in exercise 6-4 is the sensitivity of the situation that a manager like Tom Beller has to deal with. It is essential that Trina isn't intimidated into leaving the organization by the manager. He is one of the few supporters she has. This is not uncommon for the highly creative in organizations. In fact, it may be surprising that Tom even supports her. He must have many of the same traits that Trina has.

> A man with a new idea is a crank until the idea succeeds.
>
> — Mark Twain

Many organizations advertise how innovative they are; however, in most cases the word *innovative* is used because it sounds nice. When you look at these organizations, you will see they don't support highly creative people, such as Trina, who show the initiative to be creative. The question I always pose is, "How can companies be truly innovative if they don't support highly creative people?"

Most employees, including managers in the higher echelons of organizations, tend to resent stars such as Trina. Middle-of-the-road behavior and mediocre performance are preferred to displays of initiative. When a highly creative individual does step forward to advocate new and innovative ideas, he or she is viewed as a threat and is quite often ostracized by co-workers. Co-workers view him or her as a dangerous competitor who may soon be promoted ahead of them. Many managers will go out of their way to make it difficult for someone who doesn't fit the norm, despite the fact he or she adds immensely to the success and profitability of the organization, much more so than the people who fit the norm.

One of the tools managers have at their disposal to subdue highly creative people is to claim they aren't good team players. Team play has been overemphasized lately by the corporate world. Asking people to be team players results in less individualism and less creativity. In many cases managers who stress the importance of being a team player are just looking for yes-men or yes-women to work for them.

> If you have a yes-man or yes-woman working for you, one of you is redundant.
> — *Former Xerox Manager*

The individuals with the most potent ideas are the highly creative people, who are often renegades. Of course, highly creative people in general aren't good team players. Rather than try to make them team players, managers should support creative people. The bottom line is ideas don't originate from groups; ideas originate from individuals.

Many managers are looking for a yes-man or yes-woman to work for them because they are threatened by the traits of the highly creative, especially the last four traits listed on page 54. Consequently, insecure managers tend to promote people who aren't highly creative. In a *Fortune* magazine interview, Tom Watson, former CEO of then prosperous IBM, had this to say about the type of people he promoted:

> I never hesitated to promote someone I didn't like. The comfortable assistant — the nice guy you like to go on fishing trips with — is a great pitfall. Instead I looked for those sharp, scratchy, harsh, almost unpleasant guys who see and tell you about things as they really are. If you can get enough of them around you, and have patience enough to hear them out, there is no limit to where you can go.

In most large organizations a highly creative person won't be promoted. Someone who acts like an entrepreneur will be relegated or transferred to another position where he or she can no longer practice the entrepreneurial spirit. The organization either tries to tame the person or the employee is fired. Even if he or she isn't forced out, eventually, the highly creative person will realize they won't ever be supported in their creative endeavors, so they leave.

Organizations Need Highly Creative People More than the Highly Creative Need Organizations

During the present layoffs and buyouts of the corporate downsizing 1990s, which employees do you think agree to voluntarily leave organizations? It's mainly the highly creative. The confident, productive risk takers know they can function without the corporation. They consider corporate life demeaning.

The great creative individual . . . is capable of more wisdom and virtue than collective man ever can be.
— *John Stuart Mill*

Despite harsh economic conditions, more people than ever are chucking the rigid corporate world for entrepreneurial freedom or to pursue individual interests in areas personally more rewarding than their jobs. Often these "downshifters" end up making less money and working longer hours than they did in corporate life.

When a highly creative person leaves an organization, the organization is severely affected. Organizations shoot themselves in the foot, not only once or twice, but three times when they allow the highly creative to leave.

- The most obvious effect on organizations is the loss of the services of a highly innovative and productive employee.
- The second effect on the organization is the highly creative individual goes to a competitor who is much more supportive of creative people. Alternatively, the creative individual becomes the competition by starting a competing organization.
- The third serious effect on the organization, when the creative person leaves, is the remaining employees in the organization have been shown that the organization doesn't support and reward highly creative people. These employees won't see any reason to be more creative.

Corporations such as Hallmark and 3M are known for their support of the highly creative. What have innovative organizations like Hallmark and 3M found out by supporting the highly creative? The highly creative must be allowed to be themselves. They must be given their independence and given shelter. Not only should they be rewarded for success but also for failure. They must be rewarded financially with some incentive for productivity. Highly creative people tend to be very possessive of their ideas and accomplishments; they detest any other employees, especially those in higher management, taking credit for their achievements. Therefore, these stars must more than anything be given recognition for their achievements.

Art Fry, mentioned on page 48 of this chapter, was a corporate scientist with the 3M Corporation for thirty years. Fry capped a long career with 3M by developing Post-it Notes along with Spencer Silver. Without 3M's entrepreneurial encouragement, Post-it Notes would not have been developed.

In a conference speech, Art Fry stated the following about the highly creative employees or "intrapreneurs" as they are called by 3M:

Trenton, I am firing you because I can't stand obnoxious yes-men like you.

Ms. Dole, I couldn't agree with you more. What a brilliant move!

> But let me warn you. Intrapreneurs are a different breed — burrs under the saddle for many managers. They want to change things, spend money, think long term, ask embarrassing questions, challenge authority, and perhaps be disruptive. Truth, and the chance to make something happen, are often more important to them than the conventional motivations of money or power.
>
> Nevertheless, to hire those innovators and intrapreneurs, we give them time and money and freedom and a perspective of the company. We hire them to look without knowing what they will find.

In regards to these highly creative people, Leon Royer, executive director of organizational learning at 3M, states, "Either you'll learn to acquire and cultivate them, or you'll be eaten alive." Managing the highly creative is definitely not easy; once again the Easy Rule of Life applies. Highly creative individuals have to be considered high maintenance, but they are certainly worth the price. As an executive with IBM who supports highly creative people said, "One eagle is worth more than two turkeys."

> I don't want any yes-men around me. I want everybody to tell me the truth even if it costs them their jobs.
>
> — *Samuel Goldwyn*

Why Know-It-Alls Suffer from Specialist's Disease

While working on this book, I received a brochure from an international foundation; the cover states, "BE A KNOW-IT-ALL! Here's How." The inside of the brochure states, "Join our Foundation and see how easy it is to know it all." I wondered whether these people had thought about the advantages of *not* knowing it all.

There are some real problems with individuals who want to be know-it-alls. The biggest problem is that know-it-alls tend to be uncreative. Researchers have found that the more experts, or know-it-alls, think they really "know" something, the less they are open to new approaches. This is called "specialist's disease."

"Know-it-alls" or "experts" in a particular industry may con us into believing that they know more than we do about their industry because they work in that industry. Apparently, they are supposed to know what is reasonable and what isn't. Their beliefs can be liabilities. Rigid beliefs and unyielding thinking patterns have been known to stifle creativity in many fields. Elbert Hubbard defined a specialist as "one who limits himself to his chosen mode of ignorance."

In any industry the experts or specialists tend to be the least innovative. There are three things that hinder the creativity of know-it-alls:

- Knowledge
- Education
- Experience

Experts suffering from specialist's disease are master idea killers. They think they have all the reasons why something new and different will not work. Consequently, they tend to be the least creative and innovative people in their field. They also tend to be unsupportive of anyone who is trying something innovative.

> No man can be a pure specialist without being in the strict sense an idiot.
> — *George Bernard Shaw*

Specialists will give you a brilliant argument about why things won't work. And they will convince many people along the way because they are great at putting up brilliant arguments. They forget to look at one thing — why it will work!

MBA Doesn't Stand for "Mercedes-Benz Awaiting"

You need to be innovative if you want to be a leader in business today. A master's degree in business administration (MBA) may serve a purpose for many facets of business. However, if you don't have a university or college business degree, you shouldn't feel severely disadvantaged. In fact, you may actually have an advantage over someone with a degree. *Business Week* magazine recently reported most business programs stifle creativity.

Universities with business programs like the one I attended would like us to believe that MBA stands for "Mercedes-Benz Awaiting." However, as I realized after graduating with a MBA, it doesn't stand for

"Mercedes-Benz Awaiting" from creative endeavors. The average MBA graduate is not likely to be highly creative. That is why former Chrysler chairman Lee Iaccoca said, "MBAs know everything and understand nothing." When I went out into the real world, I found out what MBA really stands for. It stands for "Means Bugger All."

These are traits managers should have or things they should be good at if they wish to be successful in today's business world:

- Creativity
- Intuitive decision making
- Vision
- Zest and enthusiasm
- Ability to generate superior customer service

> You can always tell a
> Harvard man — but you
> can't tell him much.
> — *James Barnes*

How many management textbooks used at universities list all these important elements of modern management in the index? Not very many. Peter Drucker was right when he said, "When a subject becomes obsolete, universities tend to make it compulsory."

Creativity and innovation in business go beyond having university degrees. The important factors for creative success are factors you will not normally acquire in the school systems. Let's face it, some of the least creative people are individuals with MBA degrees. On the other hand, some of the most creative people in the world of business are individuals who have never heard of an MBA and won't ever need one to keep generating innovative products and services.

Beware of Specialists Who Aren't So Special

You have just discussed your new idea with the "experts" and they have stated, "It won't work." How should you react? You should find out for yourself whether your idea can be a winner. Over the years many individuals with limited knowledge, experience, and education have proved knowledgeable and experienced experts wrong.

Remember that Christopher Columbus went against the belief of the times that the world was flat. Flat-world thinking exists today, only in different forms. There have always been flat-world thinkers in all industries. Seven classic examples follow:

- Erasmus Wilson, an Oxford University professor, said in 1878, "With regard to the electric light, much has been said for and against it, but I think I may say without contradiction that when the Paris Exhibition closes, electric light will close with it, and no more will be heard of it."
- Charles Duell, director of the U.S. Patent Office, said in 1899, "Everything that can be invented has been invented."
- Harry Warner, president of Warner Brothers, in 1927 in defense of silent movies said, "Who the hell wants to hear actors talk?"
- In 1895 Lord Kelvin said, "Heavier-than-air flying machines are impossible."
- The United States National Academy of Sciences, in 1940, issued a statement declaring that there would never be such a thing as a jet aircraft: "Even considering the improvements possible — the gas turbine could hardly be considered a feasible application to airplanes, mainly because of the difficulty of complying with the stringent weight requirements."
- In 1878 Western Union rejected the exclusive rights to a new invention by stating, "What use could the company make of an electrical toy?" The new invention was the telephone.
- A president of the Michigan Savings Bank advised a lawyer not to invest in the Ford Motor Company because, "The horse is here to stay, but the automobile is only a novelty — a fad."

> A new idea is delicate. It can be killed by a sneer or a yawn: it can be stabbed to death by a quip and worried to death by a frown on the right man's brow.
>
> — *Charlie Brower*

My personal experiences have taught me to be wary of someone who tries to impress me with their vast knowledge of their industry, based on how long they have been in their occupation. I have found out that often my best bet is to be "unreasonable" and not listen to the "experts." Instead, I find out for myself what can be done and what can't be done in that industry.

After I wrote and published *The Joy of Not Working*, I received hundreds of letters, the vast majority supportive of the book. One that wasn't all that supportive was from a woman who worked as a freelance editor. She said that she agreed with a lot of the philosophy of the book; however, the book was badly written and cumbersome to read. This woman was making a proposal to rewrite the book in a more professional and academic style.

This specialist editor has two serious problems: One, she is out of touch with reality. Two, she thinks her perception of reality is the only one. Virtually everyone else who phoned me, wrote to me, or talked to me in person about *The Joy of Not Working* stated how well written and easy to read this book is. The people who contacted me included people from all walks of life, including schoolteachers and university professors. The book was even designated as required reading in a second-year leisure and recreation-studies course at the University of

> It took me fifteen years to discover that I had no talent for writing, but I couldn't give it up because by that time I was too famous.
>
> — *Robert Benchley*

Alberta. The professor who designated the book for the course told me she chose the book because the students hated most of the other books because they were so academic and difficult to read. If I had used the editor's services, the book probably would be written in such a way that the majority of readers wouldn't like it. Of course, she believed her false assumptions that everyone wants to read material that is written in a style more professional and academic than the style I chose. I wasn't about to be taken in by her false assumptions, even though she is an "expert."

It's really easy to get taken in by experts if you aren't paying attention to what's happening around you. Even the so-called best of us can be taken by the experts, and as the following example indicates, it doesn't come cheap.

This is what happened to NBC about fifteen years ago. NBC spent $750,000 (about $2 million in today's dollars) to have some creative specialists develop a new logo. Just as NBC was about to use it, they discovered, much to their dismay, that the Nebraska Educational Network, a small station in Lincoln, Nebraska, had been using almost the same logo for quite some time. NBC then paid this small station an out-of-court settlement of $55,000 in cash and $500,000 in used television equipment for the right to use this trademark. The total cost to NBC was about $1,305,000 (over $4 million in today's dollars) for the use of this trademark. Oh, by the way, the Lincoln, Nebraska, TV station paid about $100 in wages to one of its employees to develop the logo.

> A professional is a person who tells you what you know already, but in a way you cannot understand.
>
> — *Unknown Wise Person*

Some of the most important discoveries have resulted from people being totally unreasonable and defying the experts. Here are a few examples of people who have succeeded by ignoring the voice of judgment of experts.

- Anita Roddick is the founder of the Body Shop, the largest and most profitable cosmetics company in Great Britain, which also operates in Canada. The company is as well known in Britain, and almost as well known in Canada, as Coca-Cola and McDonald's are in the United States. Anita Roddick doesn't have an MBA and probably succeeded because she doesn't have one. She says, "We survived because we have no rational business knowledge." She succeeded because she didn't know it all.

- In the late 1980s, two IBM researchers, K. Alex Mueller and J. George Bednorz, disobeyed their bosses and launched a new industry by developing a practical way of creating superconductors. The incredible part of this story is that they weren't experts in this field. They worked with substances that the experts had considered to only have insulating properties and not conductivity potential. By disobeying their superiors and defying the experts, the two men won a Nobel Prize for science.

- Several years ago Jean Paré and Grant Lovig talked to major publishers about getting their first *Company's Coming* cookbook published. When the publishers weren't as interested in the book as Paré and Lovig would have liked them to be, Paré and Lovig decided to publish the cookbook on their own. Experts in the fields of writing and publishing recommend people don't publish their own books. So how did Lovig and Paré fare, not having adhered to this recommendation? Lovig, who had no experience marketing cookbooks, devised creative and unorthodox marketing strategies that the major publishers hadn't used before. The first *Company's Coming* cookbook has sold well over 800,000 copies. This is impressive, considering that out of any 65,000 books published annually in North America, only about 200 will ever see sales of 200,000 copies. Company's Coming now has 12 cookbooks with over 10 million sold to date. Paré and Lovig demonstrated there can be big payoffs from doing something with which the experts don't agree.

> An expert is a man who has stopped thinking. Why should he think? He is an expert.
> — *Frank Lloyd Wright*

The Cure for Specialist's Disease

You will benefit greatly by being able to recognize the people afflicted with "specialist's disease." Learn to ignore people who, while emphasizing their extensive experience, education, and knowledge, try to tell you that you shouldn't try something new in that industry. Follow this principle even if you are an industry newcomer.

When you undertake a new project, you will discover that many barriers appear out of nowhere. Faced with a barrier to a new project or idea, a person who focuses on experience, education, and knowledge will normally stop. The know-it-all person will now have a reason why something can't be done. You must react differently if you want to carry out your idea or project to its completion.

> Always listen to experts. They'll tell you what can't be done and why. Then do it!
>
> — *Robert Heinlein*

If your strongest trait is a healthy attitude, you are well equipped for giving it your best shot at getting your idea, service, or product successfully implemented. A healthy attitude will serve you in persevering and sticking with your project. With perseverance, you will be well on your way to eventually being a leader of the pack. Whether an idea is ultimately a success or failure, you will be a success because you gave it your best try.

Your next idea will require the same healthy attitude. Sooner or later a winning idea will emerge to make it all worthwhile. You will have left the specialists lurking in the background wondering how you, with less experience and knowledge, were able to pull it off.

Be careful that you yourself don't end up with specialist's disease where your creativity is hindered by knowledge, education, and experience. Am I saying that knowledge, education, and experience aren't valuable for creative endeavors? No! These three can be assets for our creative pursuits provided we build on them and don't use them as a substitute for creativity.

Always be prepared to listen to new ideas whether they come from peers, outsiders, or janitors. Sometimes a janitor will see a solution the highest of executives won't. The cure for specialist's disease is quite simple: Never think of yourself as a specialist. This will allow you to truly profit from the joy of not knowing it all.

> When policy fails, try thinking.
>
> — *Unknown Wise Person*

Chapter Notes

Exercise 6-4

Of course, the first step in solving the problem in this case, as in all problems, is to identify the problem (See page xviii). Is Trina the problem or is the organization the problem? In certain organizations, where structure and punctuality are important, Trina could be the problem. The solutions if Trina is the problem focus on motivating her to be on time.

Solutions If Trina Is the Problem

- This solution involves looking at the obvious. Talk to the tardy employee to find out why she is coming in late. Make a request for her to come in on time because of the implications it has to the organization.
- Institute flex-time for everyone, making it okay to be as much as one hour late, provided a full eight hours are worked by everyone.
- Offer to drive her to work.
- Make her raise contingent on consistent on-time arrival.
- Serve free coffee and doughnuts to those there on time.
- Delegate to her the responsibility of making sure that all the other employees are there on time.
- Institute early morning meetings that employees will be embarrassed to miss.
- Give her the only key to the office, with the responsibility of opening the office for everyone else, including you.
- Fire Trina and hire a less creative person to replace her.
- Change the starting time to half an hour later for everyone and see what happens.
- Allow Trina to work on a pet project for half a day a week if she comes in on time. Pet projects can generate payoffs for the corporation.
- Give Trina an opportunity to attend a seminar at a resort or prestigious location if she comes in on time for the next six months.

In most modern organizations, which must be innovative, we would have to consider the organization as the problem rather than Trina. The solutions are much different than if Trina is the problem.

Solutions If the Organization Is the Problem

- Allow her to come in late and explain to everyone else that she has earned it due to her productivity.
- Promote her further and give her executive privilege to come in late.
- Fire everyone else and hire creative employees like Trina to replace the fired ones.

- Change the culture of the organization by giving all employees seminars on the benefits of innovation and how to be more creative. Then give everyone else a chance to be creative.

- Fire Trina and then hire her back as a contract employee who does not come under normal employee regulations. Note, some big corporations in the United States are actually financially and morally supporting some of their top employees to leave the organization and start up their own businesses. The payoff is a partnership with the spin-off companies where both the parent and the infant benefit.

- Allow Trina to work at home for part of the day. Do not extend this privilege to anyone else unless they are as productive as she is.

> The function of the expert is not to be more right than other people, but to be wrong for more sophisticated reasons.
>
> — *Dr. David Butler*

CHAPTER
7

Going for It

Going for What?

If you were to walk in a clockwise direction on the walls of this figure, you would think you were going up. It would appear to you that you were destined for greater heights. However, in no time you would real-

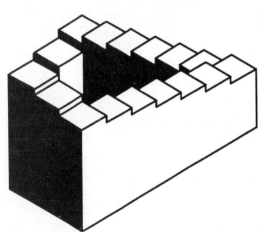

ize that you were back at the same level where you started. No matter how much energy you put into walking up the steps, higher levels would just be illusions.

Such is the illusion of activity without well-defined goals. Many people miscon-strue their unplanned activity as a direc-tion in life. They wind up putting a lot of energy into these nongoals and end up get-ting nowhere. Activity is necessary to reach greater heights, but greater heights only come with defined goals. If we are to arrive at new and worthwhile destinations, we must begin by first defining these destinations. The journey has direc-tion once the destination is set.

The most important point in defining goals is knowing where we want to go or what we want to accomplish. If there is anything that will keep us from getting what we want in life, it is not knowing what we want. Our parents want us to want certain things. Our friends want us to want. Society wants us to want. Advertisers want us to want. These are our nonwants; the question is what do we truly want for ourselves?

Why is it that many of us do not know what we want? We haven't really put much effort into finding out. Where do we want to journey? We can find this out only by taking the time to truly know ourselves. Once we get in touch with our essence, we will know what we want and where we want to go, without needing someone else to tell us what is important to us.

> It's just as difficult to reach a destination you don't have, as it is to come back from a place you've never been.
>
> — *Zig Ziglar*

Goal Setting Is Creative, Believe It or Not!

Is the setting of goals a structuring of activity? Doesn't creativity require unstructured activity? The answer to both of these questions is yes. Remember that creative success is the result of both soft and hard thinking. These two types of thinking respectively translate into unstructured and structured mental activities. By setting goals, we are adding needed structure to our mission.

Planning is important to innovation. Don't most plans fail? Yes, they do. Someone once remarked that "all plans fail and planning is invaluable." Most plans do not work out exactly the way we want them to. This means a lot of our goals will not be realized in the exact form we define, nor within the time frame we set. Nonetheless, goal setting is extremely valuable.

Goals give us something to strive for that we would not otherwise strive for. They give us a purpose. Once we have a purpose and a direction, we have reasons for being innovative and creative. It makes little sense to generate a lot of solutions without a purpose. People tend to be much more creative when they have something to work toward.

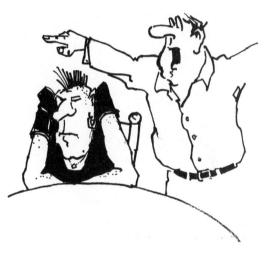

Ever think that self-discovery may lead you to a higher goal than being at lunch five years from now?

Many individuals and organizations become highly creative when a big problem or a disaster arises. They respond in creative ways because there is a need to do so. After Apple Computer, Inc. became successful with their personal computer, IBM had no choice but to invent one themselves if they wanted to tap some of this lucrative market. The goal was clear: Come up with a new personal computer in a short time frame. IBM responded by setting up a group of managers and designers who worked independently of IBM's central bureaucracy. This allowed the group to work in an environment that was conducive to innovation. The well-defined goal was what was needed to motivate IBM's managers and designers to be creative. The result was the highly successful IBM personal computer.

Why Most People Don't Go for It

Researchers say that only about 10 percent of the population in North America have well-defined goals. This may appear surprisingly low for countries that are known for their high achievers. Nonetheless, 10 percent of millions of people still translates into a large number of goal seekers. These individuals constitute the minority who are doers. They have direction and make things happen. They set important goals and attain most of them.

> Give me a stock clerk with a goal, and I will give you a man who will make history. Give me a man without a goal, and I will give you a stock clerk.
>
> — *J. C. Penny*

So how about the rest of the population? What stops the majority from investing the time to define their goals and work toward achieving them? Here are some of the reasons most people do not have goals:

- People are not convinced about the power of goal setting.
- Many people don't know what they want in life.
- Some people don't know how to set goals.
- Embarrassment is a worry for people who are afraid of failing to reach their goals.
- Some people have such a low self-image that they don't think they deserve to attain their goals.

There is one more reason. Goal setting takes effort and discipline. Once goals have been established, more effort and discipline is required in working toward the goals. Then even more effort and discipline is required to monitor the goals and set new ones. With all the effort and discipline required, many people decide against setting goals and working toward them.

Our local daily tabloid, the *Edmonton Sun,* carries a scantily dressed young woman called "Today's Sunshine Girl." The caption for Shona, a recent Sunshine Girl, read: "Fitness Instructor Shona's ambition is to get as far in life as possible — and with form like that we're sure she'll have no trouble at all." I personally think if Shona didn't define her goal much better than this, she didn't get very far toward her goal no matter how much most male readers (including me) liked her "form."

Exercise 7-1. Typical Goals That Don't Work

The following are goals that other people have set for themselves. Which of these are well-defined goals?

a) To have more money

b) To quit smoking

c) To write a book

d) To be a training specialist

e) To read more books over the next year

Like Shona's goal in life, all of the above goals can be improved upon. Well-defined goals should abide by the following principles:

Creativity Principle:

Define Your Goals

• Goals should be written down.

• Goals should be clearly defined and specific.

• Goals should be realistic, achievable, and measurable.

• Goals should have a target date and a cost limitation.

Last, goals need an action plan to get us going. It tells us what we are going to do to get to where we are going. The action plan defines the type of activity we need to follow in pursuit of our goals.

The Ultimate Goal Is Not a Goal

Ancient sayings bear out the importance of being deeply involved in the process of attaining our goals. The process is more important than the actual goal attainment. Creative people extract more enjoyment and satisfaction from their efforts than from actually reaching their goals. The satisfaction from having reached a goal, no matter how significant, is usually short lived. Many people whose major goal is to be rich are in for a big surprise. A group of New York lottery winners experienced the opposite of what most people expect from a big win. This group formed the Millionaire Circle to deal with what they called "Post-Lottery Depression Syndrome."

> I always wanted to be a somebody but I should have been more specific.
>
> — *Lily Tomlin*

Self-made millionaires tell us that goals as destinations matter less than the process itself. Most successful entrepreneurs state that getting there was most of the fun. Some businesspeople achieve their goal of financial independence and decide to take it easy. Most get bored within two or three months. They then develop new goals to pursue. Entrepreneurs seldom run out of goals because of their constant need for purpose.

All the way to heaven is heaven.

— St. Catherine of Siena

Retired people offer more evidence that the goal isn't everything. Many people who finally reach their goal of retirement find that their lives are worse than before. In fact, some retired people don't live very long after leaving the job. They become disenchanted because of their sudden loss of purpose. This absence of purpose is the result of having no more goals to pursue. Successfully retired people are not actually "retired." Retirement is another challenging process.

What's the use of running when you are on the wrong road?

— W. G. Benham

Robert Louis Stevenson said, "To travel hopefully is a better thing than to arrive." Creative people know this. When the ultimate goal becomes the process, life changes. Creativity flows more readily. Failure is viewed as success. Losing means winning. The journey becomes the destination.

Going for the Real Thing in Career Success

Sigmund Freud said work and love are the two keys to living happily as an individual. If this is the case, why are so many people who are working and married unhappy, even if they have decent marriages? The problem is, they haven't attained career success.

Exercise 7-2. Which of these are essential for career success?

- Superior intelligence
- Special skills
- Working in fields such as law, medicine, or architecture
- Luck
- Knowing the right people
- A high level of formal education
- Hard work

It may come as a surprise to you, but none of the above items is essential for career success. Millions of well-educated, richly skilled, and highly intelligent people haven't attained career success. At the same time, North America is full of hardworking people putting in ten- to fourteen-hour days who also haven't attained career success. An accountant making $30,000 a year in a dead-end job is experiencing career failure; so is a lawyer making $150,000 a year if she dislikes her profession.

What I mean by career success is getting satisfaction and enjoyment out of one's chosen work. Studies indicate that over 80 percent of people don't like what they are doing for a living. Almost 25 percent of people feel they are in "dumb" jobs for which they are overqualified. Incidentally, just in case you disagree with me and define getting rich as career success, millions of well-educated, richly skilled, and highly intelligent people, who work hard all their lives, wind up broke in retirement.

> Most people perform essentially meaningless work. When they retire that truth is borne upon them.
> — *Brendan Francis*

My premise is that career success can only be attained if you work at a job that is such a turn-on that you would work at it for free, just to experience the satisfaction from doing it. To attain job satisfaction, you need to be passionate about your work. Matthew Fox, author of *Reinvention of Work*, states:

> Work touches your heart and it has to touch other people's hearts.
> If there's one question I would ask to awaken us to spiritual work,
> it would be: "How does your work touch the joy in you and what joy
> does your work bring out in others?"

When your work is your passion, there is no distinction between work and play. In the old concept of work, you won't have to "work" another day in your life. But I can't decide for you what your passion is; you have to do this yourself.

The reason so many people from the baby-boom generation are suffering from midlife crises is they never pursued a job or career that was their passion. During the 1980s, most of these people pursued careers or jobs that paid the most money, so they could live the yuppie lifestyle of excess materialism. They may have achieved career success as they defined the term. They got to the top of the corporate ladder and acquired their material possessions. However, their marriages may be in shambles, their children are all messed up, and they themselves are suffering from excessive stress and dissatisfaction.

What is essential for their career success is working at something they enjoy; they must be serving others in a positive way. An enriched life won't be available to those dissatisfied workers who switch jobs, unless they find a job that coincides with, or supports, their personal mission. More important than economic factors in job selection should be the issue of lifestyle or quality of life. A balance between work and personal life is much more important than acquiring more money and material possessions than everyone else.

The biggest obstacle to people achieving career success is a lack of self-esteem. Most people are held captive by programming about what success means to their parents or to society. Many people unhappy in their careers are working at unsuitable jobs because they are trying to fulfill someone else's dream, instead of their own. At the extreme, many employees are so miserable that they are suffering from ongoing job-related stress.

> The longer the title, the less important the job.
> — George McGovern

If you have a mediocre job, more money isn't the answer. The idea "If I was paid more in my job, then I would be happier with what I do" is a myth. The opposite is often true. If you were happier with what you do, you would make more money. If your job has little connection with your values and real interests, you will feel dissatisfied regardless of how much money you make.

You should try to find work that enriches your body and mind. You want to be rewarded for your work with praise, raises, promotions, and room for growth. Your job should give you some level of control and flexibility. Finding creative employment should be your goal. Do what you like or what you are. If you are artistic or a good leader, try to put these talents to use in your career. You have to be somewhat realistic. It's a case of being creative and doing the most with what you have.

When choosing a career related to your purpose or mission, you need to be aware of your aspirations. Listen to your inner voice, and not to what others tell you to do or be. If your work is your passion, you will be highly motivated to achieve great things, and your chances for monetary success will be enhanced.

> Be what you is, not what you ain't, 'cause if you ain't what you is, you is what you ain't.
> — Luther D. Price

Workplaces can be exciting, challenging, active, stimulating, and innovative. They can also be dull, routine, frustrating, dejecting, and boring. You must choose your employer wisely. Make sure that your job is enjoyable and satisfying and that you have room to grow and learn. You want to be valued for your new ideas, your positive energy, and your ability to be productive.

If you have recently been downsized, or are about to be, this may be a blessing in disguise. You may be able to turn a negative situation into a positive one. Now may be the time to challenge your need for security and fear of risk. Searching for a regular job may appear to be the safe way out, but you may be selling yourself short. This may be the opportune time to pursue something that is creative and fulfilling. Sure, there is the fear of the unknown, but finding another regular job carries the risk that you may be downsized again in six months or a year. You may attain much more security by pursuing a career with your personal mission in mind. If you get established in a business of your own, you won't ever have to consider working for anyone else again.

As a writer and professional speaker, I can vouch for the advantages of not working for someone else. Having paid the price of searching for and discovering what I want to do, I am doing what I enjoy most on my terms. There is no life like it — what a great way to make a living! Why work for any one of millions of bosses when I can work for my favorite boss — *me*? As mentioned before, I only ask that I work four hours a day. I also give myself permission to avoid working in any month that doesn't have an *r* in it. By working less, I may not make a lot of money compared to what I could make working twelve hours a day. However, it's all relative. My income looks really good to the employees who work at the local car wash.

> Write without pay until somebody offers pay. If nobody offers within three years, the candidate may look upon this circumstance with the most implicit confidence as the sign that sawing wood is what he was intended for.
>
> — *Mark Twain*

Breaking away from conventional employment by working for yourself in your own business, or as a contract employee, gives you more opportunity to attain job satisfaction. One advantage is that you don't have someone telling you what to do. You have control over your workplace and flexibility in when and how you work.

The key to a satisfying career is to utilize your special talents at something you love. Ron Smotherman, in his book *Winning Through Enlightenment,* stated, "Satisfaction is for a very select group of people: those who are willing to be satisfied. There aren't many around." Do you want to be in the select group of people who are satisfied in their work? If the answer is yes, then you have to keep asking yourself these important questions: What are you good at? What are your talents? How about your strengths and weaknesses? Which would you like to use and improve in a career? Would you ever do a certain type of work for free just for the enjoyment? Keep asking yourself these questions every day for the next year if you have to. The answers may eventually lead you into work that you can be passionate about.

Following is the content of a letter I received from Linda W., a woman from Toronto who decided to quit her secure job with the Ontario government and move to the interior of British Columbia after having read *The Joy of Not Working.*

Ernie, Ernie, Ernie,

Just finished reading *The Joy of Not Working* and I love it! You gave me the little boost that I needed with regards to pulling up stakes and heading to B.C.

I'm a part-time writer, public speaker, spiritual to the core and I have decided to head for the mountains of B.C. (even though there is a recession/depression), say to hell with the b.s. of a government office, good-bye concrete city and I am out of here.

You gave me that little something that said "go for it kid, you are not a fool to find peace of mind."

Yours truly,

Linda W.

Note that Linda W. didn't use any of these excuses: "There is a recession," "I can't leave a secure government job," or "I don't have the education for starting in a new field." She listened to her inner voice, which told her it was time to go. I am sure that she experienced at least some fear. She handled the fear by confronting it. She knew that she had to take risks if she was to experience some adventure and live life to the fullest.

Somewhere along the way, you may have had a sense of what you really would love to do. Instead, you chose a career or job considerably different from what could have been your passion. Over the years, you may have repressed this dream of a career with a higher purpose, because you concluded it was an unattainable fantasy. Now is the time to explore your dreams and wildest fantasies to give you some clues as to what you should be pursuing for a career.

> Live your beliefs and you can turn the world around.
> — *Henry David Thoreau*

When you are doing what you want to do, the things you enjoy and the things you are good at, life becomes much easier. There are at least four reasons for this: First, you get satisfaction in life. Second, you get to be very good at what you do. Third, money comes easier. Fourth, you feel good about how you earn your money.

Life without Purpose Is Life without Direction

In his book *The Master Game*, D. S. DeRopp stated, "Seek above all for a game worth playing. Such is the oracle to modern man. Having found the game, play it with intensity, play as if your life and sanity depend on it. (They do depend on it.)"

Contributing to the world in a meaningful way helps us earn self-respect and the respect of others. The longing for meaning and purpose in our lives is normal. A sense of usefulness is essential for your satisfaction in life, especially as you grow older. Be clear about who you are and what you want out of life. You should have a reason to get up in the morning. When you have a true purpose or personal mission, you have a sense that you are making a difference in the lives of others.

> The world is full of willing people. Some willing to work, the rest willing to let them.
>
> — *Robert Frost*

No one's life needs to lack purpose. You have to discover or create your own purpose if you want to feel that you are making a real difference in this world. You have to tap your creativity to discover your purpose.

Not having discovered your personal life mission at thirty or forty years of age doesn't mean you won't find it. Many people haven't discovered what they really wanted to do until midlife or later. Regardless of how old you are, it is never too late to reinvent yourself, discover your mission, and pursue it with vigor. If you need an education to arrive at a career that will coincide with your mission, then get it. An excuse that arises is, "But I am forty-nine and I will be fifty-three when I get there." In four years, you are going to be fifty-three anyway. If you don't do what you have to, you will be fifty-three and just as dissatisfied, or possibly more dissatisfied, than you are today. Your personal mission will surface if you are ready for it. Here are three examples of people involved in a personal mission at a later age:

- Before his death in 1997 at the age of eighty-four, Red Skelton showed much more zest for life than most people in their twenties and thirties. Why? He had a personal mission to entertain people and make them happy. Skelton got only three hours of sleep, going to bed at 2:30 A.M. and rising at 5:30 A.M. He spent his time writing stories, composing music, and painting. After he turned eighty, he still averaged seventy-five live performances a year.

- Martin Miller of Indiana, at ninety-seven, was working full-time lobbying for the rights of senior citizens.

- Mary Baker Eddy was eighty-seven when she followed her personal mission — starting a new newspaper with a religious influence. She called it the *Christian Science Monitor*.

You must not stop pursuing goals just to please or compete with others. The key is to create a purpose that you are passionate about. If you can establish some ultimate mission in your life, you will have a fiery driving force to keep your life exciting and interesting. This will ensure you are constantly growing and learning.

Discovering your purpose is the cornerstone for using your personal creativity. The biggest challenge will be looking within, discovering your purpose, and living out that purpose. Your life should never be without purpose. Your personal mission should relate to your essence and your dreams. Being on purpose means each task, act, and situation will be worthy of your total attention. Discovering your personal mission will give you a direction in life that is truly your own.

Do not let what you cannot do interfere with what you can do.
— *John Wooden*

If you last defined your goals sometime ago, they may have changed with time, as did the goals of Linda W. who wrote the above letter. Now may be a good time to review your goals and decide what you want to do with your life.

It is your challenge, and not anyone else's, to find, accept, and develop who you can be as an individual. You must face reality and accept that absolutely everything worth attaining in life — adventure, a relaxed mind, love, spiritual fulfillment, satisfaction, and happiness — has a price. Anything that enhances your existence will take action and effort. If you think otherwise, you will be in for much frustration.

Remember that it is more satisfying to climb mountains than to slide down them sitting on your butt. Sitting around waiting for someone else to light the fire doesn't work. Lighting your own fire, instead of waiting around to be warmed by someone else's, will make this lifetime (and other lifetimes beyond this one if you believe in reincarnation) worth living.

In the Land of the Blind, One Eye Is King

You Can Observe a Lot Just by Watching

It is always interesting to hear what participants in my seminars and courses see in the above figure. Some participants don't see anything. What do you see in it?

A consultant to restaurants in Western Canada makes a good living by saving restaurant operations from having to declare bankruptcy. What does he do that the owners are not able to do? Not much except that he is able to see the obvious. The consultant spots inefficiencies such as too many entrées on the menu. He may also see staff and equipment tied up in unproductive activities.

Changes are made that could be recommended by just about anyone except by those directly associated with the restaurant. Many of these restaurants are saved because the obvious problems are pointed out to the owners. Without the consultant, they would not see the obvious and the restaurants would go into receivership.

Many times the best solutions are right before our eyes and we don't see them. The obvious escapes us. Yogi Berra said it well: "You can observe a lot just by watching."

> The best way to
> make your dreams
> come true is to
> wake up.
> — Paul Valery

A character in Joseph Heller's *Catch 22* had flies in his eyes. He couldn't see these flies in his eyes. Reason: The flies in his eyes prevented him from seeing these same flies in his eyes. Often we are like this character.

Incidentally, there is a bicycle in the previous figure. Once you know it is there, try and not see it. Many things are this way. We won't see the obvious. However, once it is pointed out to us, we can't help but see it.

Exercise 8-1 has an answer that is obvious, yet easy to overlook. Allow yourself thirty seconds to do the exercise.

Exercise 8-1. Winning by Being the Slowest

A rather eccentric businessman wants to bequeath his financial empire and personal wealth to one of his two sons. He decides that a horse race will be run by the two sons. The son who owns the slower horse will become the owner of everything. Each son fears that the other will cheat by having his horse go slower than it is capable of going. Both of the sons approach a wise old philosopher for his advice. The philosopher, without much delay, tells them in two words how to make sure the race will be fair. What are the two words?

If you are one of the two sons, is there something else you can do to ensure you win the empire?

(See Chapter Notes, page 83, for solutions.)

Why Didn't I Think of That?

Following are several examples of creative individuals who have profited from seeing solutions that have many other people saying, "Why didn't I think of that?"

- How about starting a newsletter for which the subscribers send you most of the material? Amy Dacyczyn set aside her career in graphic design to become a mother. In seven years, by saving money rather than earning more, Amy and her husband, on an income of less than $30,000 a year still had saved over $49,000 for a house, made major purchases of $38,000, and were completely debt free. They achieved this even though they had four children to support. Thrifty Amy was known as the Frugal Zealot to her friends. Over time she became irked by seemingly intelligent people on daytime talk shows expounding myths such as "Nowadays, a family has to have two incomes to make ends meet" and "Nowadays, families cannot get into the housing market." In June of 1990, Amy started *The Tightwad Gazette,* a newsletter that promotes thrift as a viable alternative lifestyle. She saw subscriptions climb to over 100,000 in two years. Because Amy doesn't consider her knowledge about thrift to be well rounded, she solicits reader participation. This provides a great source of fresh material to keep her newsletter interesting and loaded with new ideas.

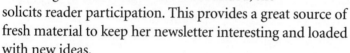

Creativity Principle:

Look for the Obvious

- David Chilton markets information, which he labels as "nothing new," in a new way. In the late 1980s, Chilton, a stockbroker and financial planner, encountered a problem. He gave his clients various books on financial planning and investing. However, he discovered, much to his disappointment, most clients didn't get around to reading these books. The books all blitzed the readers with boring statistics, graphs, and charts. This is when Chilton decided to write about the basic principles of personal finance and investing in a unique fashion. He took a complex topic and presented it in a reader-friendly way when he wrote *The Wealthy Barber.* Commercial publishers rejected the idea of his book on finance, which reads like fiction. So Chilton self-published the book. When he had shown that the book was a hit, a commercial publisher took it over. *The Wealthy Barber* has now sold over 1 million copies and continues to sell at a torrid rate. Chilton's book, which takes an unconventional approach to a conventional topic, has had many other financial planners saying, "Why didn't I think of that?"

> It requires a very unusual mind to undertake the analysis of the obvious.
>
> — *Alfred North Whitehead*

- Robert Plath, a former Northwest Orient pilot, was required to carry more than forty pounds of manuals with him on every flight. Being a little lazy, he screwed a cart to his carry-on bag. Other pilots figured he was a wimp. Being a wimp — an observant one — had its payoff. Plath invented the Travelpro Rollaboard suitcase with wheels and a retractable handle. Although there were already bag and cart combinations on the market, they didn't look very good to Plath. So he designed his own prototype and had it manufactured in mass quantities in Asia. At first he received a cold response to his invention, which the retail market scoffed at. Plath started by selling his units to his former airline colleagues through mail order. In due time retail outlets were begging for his product. It was introduced around 1989 and has had sales of $30 million since then. Industry observers of the luggage industry now call Plath's Rollaboard the biggest invention in more than fifteen years.

- In the 1800s, bicycle manufacturers overlooked the obvious solution for years. The design of the bicycle first featured two wheels the same size but over time the front wheel got larger and larger. Initially the pedal assembly was attached directly on the front wheel. To make bicycles faster, the front wheel had to be increased in size. Bicycles became rather cumbersome. The solution to this problem was before the industry's eyes. One day someone noticed something that was used in the manufacture of bicycles that could be used on the bicycles as well. It was a drive-train assembly. This person thought, "Why not use it to power the rear wheel?" It was only a matter of time before the bicycle was made with two wheels the same size.

> Common sense is not very common.
>
> — *Latin Proverb*

- Howard Schultz turned an everyday product into a customer craze. Although coffee sales declined since the 1960s due to health concerns, Schultz has elevated Starbucks, the Seattle-based gourmet coffee company, into one of the most rapid-growing businesses in North America. In the 1980s, Schultz visited Italy on a coffee-buying trip and saw the romantic relationship Italians have with coffee. Schultz decided to build a national chain of Starbucks patterned after the Italian coffee bars. He adapted coffee to the American palate by creating offerings such as espresso both straight and diluted. Now it is not uncommon for dedicated customers in places like Seattle and Vancouver to spend $100 a month or more at Starbucks coffee bars.

Exercises with Obvious Solutions That Are Not So Obvious to Most People

(Solutions to the exercises are in the Chapter Notes, page 83.)

Exercise 8-2. Matching Socks in the Dark

Five months ago a man threw away all his old socks and purchased ten pairs of identical black socks and four pairs of identical brown socks. Since then he has lost three of the black socks and one brown sock. Assume there is a power failure in the evening just as he is about to go out. He is fully dressed except he does not have on his socks and shoes.

Unable to see in the darkness of his bedroom, what is the minimum number of socks the man has to remove from his dresser drawer to ensure that he has a matching pair?

> If your mind is empty, it is always ready for anything; it is open to everything. In the beginner's mind there are many possibilities; in the expert's mind there are few.
>
> — *Shunryu Suzuki,* Zen Mind, Beginner's Mind

Exercise 8-3. The Obvious on the Typewriter Keyboard

Q W E R T Y U I O P

As you may already know, the above is the top row of the typewriter keyboard. First here is some trivia about the typewriter; the layout of the keyboard was designed in the 1800s to slow typists down because they were jamming up the mechanical keys when typing too fast. We now have more efficient keyboards, which are compatible with the faster electronic typewriters. People have not accepted the new layouts because of resistance to change, another block to creativity and innovation.

So much for the trivia. What is the longest word that you can make in the English language with the top row of the typewriter keyboard?

Exercise 8-4. Finding the Fastest Way

As president of Superior Time Air, you have just had a hectic week trying to get a number of projects completed. Time Air has regular scheduled flights to about 20 percent of the cities in Canada and the United States. One of the projects involves your Charter Holiday Service. This is a new service just introduced to serve all of North America.

Your airline has just had 15,000 brochures printed, which are slated to be put in travel agencies in all major cities across North America.

You are trying to figure the fastest way for you to get these brochures out to all the agents. The peak holiday season is about to start, and every minute counts.

Being a creative manager, how are you going to get these brochures to their destinations in the fastest possible time?

Exercise 8-5. Dressing for Success

A U.S. bank realized that it needed to improve its image. One of the problems that needed attention was getting the employees to dress better. The bank was very concerned with what the reaction of the employees would be if a dress code was imposed by senior management. The bank management was able to resolve the problem with little resistance from the employees. What do you think they did?

Exercise 8-6. Why Aren't They Having Any Fun?

As the new manager of community facilities in a large city, you have noticed that children are not playing in the playgrounds. Someone has told you that children find playgrounds boring. What can you do about this problem?

Exercise 8-7. The Graffiti Puzzle

Two years ago, while cycling in a residential area I cycle through regularly, I came upon an old Ford truck with the box built up on the sides and a tailgate made from four boards. Painted on the tailgate was some graffiti as indicated on the above drawing.

For the next two weeks I cycled in this area and kept seeing the graffiti on the back of this truck. I figured if this was my truck I would be creative and turn the boards of the tailgate upside down or inside out to make the graffiti unreadable.

However I missed an obvious solution, which the owner eventually used to eliminate the graffiti problem. Can you see the obvious solution?

Exercise 8-8. Milk It for All You Can

A kid in school was asked by the teacher to name seven things with milk in them. The boy gave the teacher his answer in ten seconds. Can you answer this in ten seconds?

Exercise 8-9. Easy to Miss the Boat

A man is sailing in a boat at ten knots against a wind, which is gusting at five knots. The man is thirty-eight years old. His boat weighs 98 pounds, and he weighs 152 pounds. What nationality is the man?

Chapter Notes

Exercise 8-1

The two words are *Change horses.* For the second part of the exercise, you can shoot your horse to make it the slowest.

Exercise 8-2

To get a matching pair, the man only need take out three socks.

Exercise 8-3

Don't overlook the obvious. Try the word *typewriter.*

Exercise 8-4

As president you should practice a fundamental principle of management: *Delegate* — to the head of the mailroom or the person in charge of these types of tasks.

Exercise 8-5

The new dress code was enthusiastically received by the employees because senior management "gave the problem away." Instead of dictating a policy themselves, management named a committee of employees to come up with a policy. The employees proposed a satisfactory dress code after their research.

Exercise 8-6

Get children involved in the design of your playgrounds.

Exercise 8-7
Hint: Consider the make of truck. If you still can't get it, see Appendix, page 180.

Exercise 8-8
The boy's answer was butter, cheese, ice cream, and four cows.

Exercise 8-9
The sailor is Chinese. Why? Okay, the solution is not that obvious but why he is Chinese is very obvious. (See Appendix, page 180.)

CHAPTER 9

Thinking Way Out in Left Field

Seeing Double or Better

As a young lawyer, Abraham Lincoln one day had to plead two similar cases. He happened to get the same judge for both cases and both cases involved the same principle of law. In the case heard in the morning Lincoln appeared for the defendant. He made an eloquent plea and easily won his case. Ironically, in the case heard in the afternoon Lincoln happened to be acting for the plaintiff. Lincoln was arguing this case with the same eagerness, only from the opposite point of view, when the judge, somewhat amused, asked Lincoln why he had changed his attitude since the morning. Lincoln replied, "Your Honor, I could have been wrong this morning, but I know I'm right this afternoon."

> The realization that there are other points of view is the beginning of wisdom.
> — *Charles M. Campbell*

The moral of this true story is don't get stuck in your beliefs. This can come back to haunt you. Structured thinking limits your ability to see things in a different light; instead, learn to be a flexible thinker. Go as far as possible to be a divergent thinker on a regular basis.

Most of us have a tendency to structure our thinking patterns in ways that prevent us from seeing all the possibilities there are for finding solutions to life's problems. This tendency has a great impact on our creative abilities.

Test your flexibility in thinking with the following exercise:

Exercise 9-1. What Is Going On Here?

Betty, a forty-two-year-old schoolteacher, bought her daughter, Milisa, a new bicycle for her sixth birthday. On this day Milisa was riding the bicycle in front of an office building when she was struck by a car and injured. The police and ambulance were called and both arrived on the scene shortly after. The six-year-old girl was not injured seriously but the ambulance attendants decided to have her lie down on the stretcher so that she could be taken to the hospital for observation. Just as they were putting the little girl in the ambulance, a twenty-eight-year-old clerk-typist ran out of the building and screamed, "That's Milisa! What happened to my daughter?"

Whose daughter is Milisa, the schoolteacher's or the clerk-typist's?

To find the most logical solution to exercise 9-1, most of us require a breaking away from structured thinking patterns. In retrospect the solution is obvious (see Chapter Notes, page 95). Yet the logical solution escapes many of us due to our set mind patterns.

> The guy who invented the first wheel was an idiot. The guy who invented the other three, he was a genius.
>
> — Sid Caesar

Flexibility in thinking requires mainly effort on the thinker's part. Researchers have found that most successful people in business have developed the habit of thinking in flexible or nonlinear terms. This results in innovative ways of marketing products, financing projects, or managing employees. These people see double or better in business.

Divergent thinking leads to more opportunities for people than does linear or vertical thinking. *Lateral thinking*, a term coined by Edward de Bono, is another term for divergent thinking. This mode of thinking goes beyond the rational and traditional.

Attempt solving the problem in exercise 9-2 with lateral thinking.

Exercise 9-2. The Flagpole Dilemma

You are the manager of a McDowers hamburger outlet in the United States. McDowers is the largest chain of its kind in the world. Charles Block is the owner and demands excellence from his managers.

The time period is the late sixties. Four days ago a large riot resulted after a demonstration was held at Bent State University. The United States Army was called in to assist state police. In the confusion that resulted, soldiers started shooting and killed four students. Anger and outrage have been expressed all over America, especially in universities and colleges.

After listening to the news on the radio, you drive into work and start your day. You work until noon and then take a break. Listening to the news on the radio, you hear that marches are being held in all major cities and towns in the states and students are demanding all American flags be flown at half-mast. You think about the flagpole in front of your McDowers outlet and the American flag on it. It occurs to you that it is a good thing no marchers are in front of your establishment. Charles Block, your boss, would think it unpatriotic to fly the flag at half-mast because of an act the soldiers committed in the line of duty. In fact, you know Mr. Block would fire you if he knew that you bowed to the students' demands and flew your flag at half-mast.

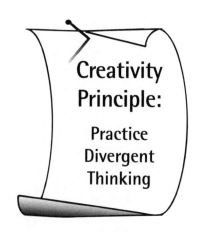

Creativity Principle:

Practice Divergent Thinking

At 2:00 in the afternoon, your assistant informs you that, a quarter of a mile away, there are 2,000 students on their way to your hamburger outlet, demanding that you show your respect for the deceased. They want you to personally go out and lower the flag to half-mast. Television crews and newspaper reporters are accompanying the angry students.

At this point it becomes very clear that if you do not lower the flag, the students will probably destroy a good part of your building. Charles Block will not be too happy about this. It is likely he will fire you if this happens. On the other hand he will probably fire you if you personally lower the flag since, in his opinion, this would be unpatriotic.

What will be your course of action?

Exercise 9-3. Paper Clips for What?

You're the manager of a manufacturing company that, by mistake, made several million boxes of paper clips for which you have no market. These paper clips are now taking up valuable storage space. What alternatives do you have for disposing of the paper clips?

Exercise 9-2 is based upon a real-life situation to which a manager had to react. If your decision was either to lower the flag for the students or to refuse to do so and suffer the consequences of having property damaged, your decision was based on vertical thinking. Divergent thinking was used by the manager who faced this situation in real life (see Chapter Notes, page 95). His response saved him his job. There are several nonlinear solutions to this situation. Can you come up with at least three original ones?

Exercise 9-3 isn't best solved with only linear or vertical thinking. Linear solutions are those that are rational and traditional. One linear solution is to sell the paper clips at the least possible financial loss. Vertical thinking is straightforward thinking that involves careful logical analysis of the solution. Vertical thinkers will think only in terms of getting rid of the paper clips to organizations that want paper clips to clip papers together.

This sign works a lot better than *Private Beach, No Swimming.*

A divergent thinker who attempts exercise 9-3 will think not only in terms of disposing the paper clips to minimize losses, but also in terms of finding new uses for the paper clips. Divergent thinkers will explore all the different ways of using paper clips, rather than just exploring the most logical and promising uses for them. Divergent thinking has to do with new ways of looking at things and generating new ideas of every sort imaginable. In my seminars we do an exercise to show that the uses for paper clips are literally unlimited.

So, remember to move your thoughts from being rigid and focused to a state of being different and interesting. Exercise 9-4, along with the various mind benders, provides further practice in divergent thinking. Be sure to look for ideas that stem from the nonlinear approach as well as the linear approach.

The art of being wise is the art of knowing what to overlook.
— William James

Exercise 9-4. Queen of Stones

Once upon a time, there lived a widowed queen who was selfish, jealous, and ugly. She had a beautiful daughter who was loved by a young handsome prince. The princess was in love with the prince as much as the prince was in love with her. They decided to get married but had to get permission from the queen.

The queen also fancied the prince and wanted to marry him. So wealthy was the queen that her garden path was littered with diamonds and rubies. She was willing to give all her wealth to the prince if the prince married her; however, the prince only wanted the princess.

One fine afternoon while the three of them were strolling along the garden path, the queen proposed that they let chance decide who shall marry the prince. She stated that she would choose a ruby and a diamond from the path and put them in a jewelry box. Without looking, the princess would have to pick one of the precious stones from the box. If she chose the diamond the queen would marry the prince and if she chose the ruby the princess would be the lucky one to marry the prince.

The young prince and the princess reluctantly consented to this proposal. As the queen stooped to pick up two stones, the princess noticed that the unscrupulous queen selected two diamonds, instead of a ruby and a diamond, and placed them in the jewelry box. She then asked the princess to choose one of the two stones from the box without looking.

What should the princess do under the circumstances? (See Chapter Notes, page 96, for solutions.)

Mind Benders to Run Your Brain off Its Rails

Puzzles force us to think in new ways by challenging the way we think about ideas, numbers, shapes, and words. Try these mind benders to practice your divergent thinking. (Solutions are in Chapter Notes, beginning on page 96.)

Mind Bender 1. Half of 13 Is Not Always 6.5

Use your flexibility in thinking to generate at least seven solutions to "What Is Half of Thirteen?"

Mind Bender 2. What Is the Prime Minister Up To?

The prime minister of Canada has just about completed remodeling the outside of his residence in Ottawa. He still needs something to finish the job. He goes down to the hardware store and looks at what he needs to finish the job. If the prime minister of Britain bought these items for his official residence in London, one would cost him $2.99 and ten would cost him $5.98.

The prime minister of Canada chose to buy twenty-four. The clerk charged him $5.98, the same as the prime minister of Britain would be charged for ten. What did the prime minister of Canada buy?

> A man must have a certain amount of intelligent ignorance to get anywhere.
>
> — *Charles F. Kettering*

Mind Bender 3. Rain, Rain, Don't Need to Go Away

For thirty-five minutes a thirty-eight-year-old man walked through a severe rainstorm. He didn't wear a hat, had no umbrella, and didn't hold anything over himself while he was in the rain. Yet he didn't get even one hair on his head wet during these thirty-five minutes. How was he able to do this?

Mind Bender 4. The Chicken or the Egg

A farmer living on the prairies eats four eggs a day for breakfast. He hasn't had any chickens on the farm for two years. He doesn't beg, borrow, steal, or buy the eggs and no one ever gives him anything. Where does the farmer get his eggs?

Mind Bender 5. A New Coin?

A child goes to the store with two coins that add up to thirty cents. One of the coins is not a nickel. What are the two coins that the child has?

Mind Bender 6. Long and Short Months

Seven months of the year have thirty-one days. How many have thirty days?

Mind Bender 7. Becoming Smaller by Being Bigger

Can you think of three different words that become smaller if you add letters to them?

Mind Bender 8. Wet Behind the Ears

Anthropologists on an excavating expedition were looking for artifacts when one of the junior members excitedly yelled that he had found a gold coin marked 6 B.C. The leader of the expedition took one look at it and said it was not made in 6 B.C. Being one not to tolerate stupidity, the leader fired the junior member on the spot. Why?

Mind Bender 9. Younger Than She Looks

A woman is celebrating her tenth birthday. On the same day her daughter who is twenty is getting married. How can this be?

Mind Bender 10. Creating One Out of Five

A man wants to join five chains, each with four links, into one closed chain. To open a link will cost $1.00 and to close a link will cost $1.50. He was able to create a single closed chain for less than $11.00. How was he able to do this?

Rebus Mind Benders

Here is a whole new batch of rebus exercises I created to help you develop your ability to think divergently. Can you determine what the following rebuses stand for. Example: LVS stands for Elvis.

> Great innovators and original thinkers and artists attract the wrath of mediocrities as lightning rods draw the flashes.
>
> — *Theodor Reik*

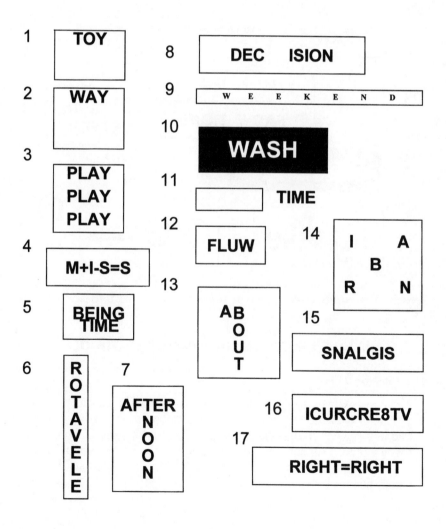

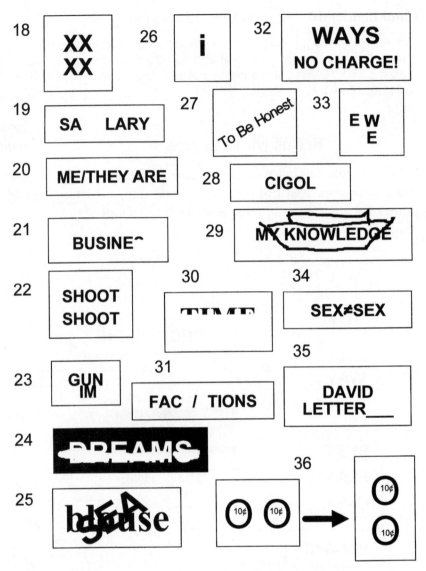

18 XX XX	26 i	32 **WAYS** NO CHARGE!
19 SA LARY	27 To Be Honest	33 E W E
20 ME/THEY ARE	28 CIGOL	
21 BUSINE^	29 MY KNOWLEDGE	
22 SHOOT SHOOT	30 ~~TIME~~	34 SEX≠SEX
23 GUN IM	31 FAC / TIONS	35 DAVID LETTER___
24 ~~DREAMS~~		
25 b̶e̶c̶a̶u̶s̶e̶	36	

See Chapter Notes, page 97, when you are finished with these.

More Exercises for Divergent Minds

Exercise 9-5

About three years ago the Doonesbury cartoon strip showed a color picture of the U.S. flag with the main cartoon figure looking at the flag and saying, "Kids, here's a real brainteaser! Try disposing of today's comics section without violating George Bush's proposed constitutional amendment on flag desecration. Sure the flag is only paper, but it's still the U.S. symbol."

He goes on to say, "No using it to line a birdcage or train a puppy — that's desecration! No throwing it in the garbage and no using it to start a fire in the fireplace — that's flag burning! Good Luck. Then he goes on to say, "Solution? There is none! You're stuck with this flag until it crumbles! Sorry, kids, but that's the way it goes."

I disagree that there is no solution. Can you figure out a solution to this problem? I certainly can. (See Chapter Notes, page 96, for my solution.)

Exercise 9-6

In 1990 Dick Barr, president of Western Mortgage (Realty) Corp., had a problem with the parking lot in the company's office building on West Broadway in Vancouver. Virtually all the spots were reserved and big signs were posted saying vehicles would be towed away. The problem was people would park in the reserved stalls. By the time a tow truck could be summoned, the culprits had left.

Dick Barr used divergent thinking and came up with an inexpensive solution that reduced most of the illegal parking.

What would you do in a similar situation? (See Chapter Notes, page 96, for Barr's solution.)

Divergent Thinking in Action

Great leaders in business regularly use divergent or nonlinear thinking in their decision making. Many experts on management claim that the use or the lack of use of divergent thinking separates successful managers from the less successful ones. Divergent thinking involves being way out in left field.

We all can develop the ability to be more innovative and divergent in our thinking. The payoffs can be big. Here are just a few examples of the payoffs enjoyed as a result of divergent or left-field thinking used by these people in business.

- Canadian Ron Foxcroft spent three years developing a new whistle for referees. He finally perfected his whistle, with its distinctive, piercing pitch, but for months after, he didn't sell a single whistle in Canada. He said he kept running into negativity, and not one sporting-goods store in the many he approached bought a whistle. The owners of one sporting-goods store refused to take the whistle on consignment because it was the dumbest thing they had ever seen.

Faced with a big problem, Foxcroft resorted to divergent thinking. At the Pan-American Games held in Indianapolis, Foxcroft stayed up until the middle of the night and then blew his whistle like never before in the dormitory grounds where 400 referees, judges, and linesmen were sleeping.

Foxcroft woke up most of the officials, but it paid off. The next day he took orders for 20,000 of his Foxcroft 40 whistle, at $6.00 each. Today his whistle is used by lifeguards, snowmobilers, skiers, and officials in every major league except hockey.

> It's them who take advantage that get advantage in this world.
> — *George Eliot*

• In 1996 Barclay's Bank in Madrid, Spain, had a problem with customers' complaints about the danger when using the bank's automatic money-dispensing machines. The problem was the shelters for the money-dispensing machines were being used at night by the homeless and prostitutes, who were scaring off the bank's customers. The bank solved the problem using some lateral thinking. It installed infrared motion sensors and a loudspeaker message advising, "Our concern for your security is increasing. If you don't use the automatic teller machine or leave the lobby within fifteen seconds, we will call the police for your safety."

> Some fellows get credit for being conservative when they are only stupid.
> — *Kin Hubbard*

• In the late 1980s, Barry Kukes of Compu-Pak increased his sales of floppy diskettes 100 percent in just five months, to an annual rate of two million dollars. How did he do it? By using "new" and "different" packaging. His first hit was the "swimsuit" floppy diskette, which featured a bikini-clad woman on the label. He came up with puppy dog labels and intends to use cars along with some other objects in future packaging. Kukes wasn't worried that his packaging did not make any sense. "What does a girl in a swimsuit have to do with a floppy diskette?" you ask. His answer: "We'll be the first to admit, absolutely nothing."

Because of his unusual packaging, Kukes received substantial free publicity. If you want to receive free publicity, remember that the media are not in the business of promoting your product. The people in the media want a good story. Practice divergent thinking. Be first, be daring, and be different, and the media will write about you and your business.

MR. BOFFO

- In 1989 Hy's Encore Restaurant in Vancouver was faced with the problem of potential customers thinking that the restaurant was closed. On each side of the restaurant a high-rise building was being demolished, making it look like the two-story restaurant building was being demolished as well.

  The restaurant took out an advertisement in the *Vancouver Sun*, which showed a picture of Hy's with the buildings being demolished on both sides. The advertisement read:

  Hy's Encore Operating At Full Blast - Despite rumors to the contrary this landmark, amid all the construction activity on Hornby Street, is still open and operating at its twenty-seven-year location. Major renovations to the premises are almost complete, providing a stunning new look for customers. Pictured is the first phase of the renovation program which included demolition of adjacent buildings.

Chapter Notes

Exercise 9-1
Note how easy it is for the majority of us to structure our thinking. Although there can be more than one answer to this, the most logical answer is Milisa is the daughter of both the schoolteacher and the clerk-typist. The clerk-typist happens to be a man married to an older woman. (Only about 20 percent of seminar participants get this.)

Exercise 9-2
Many solutions are available from lateral thinkers. One of my solutions was to delegate to an assistant manager and get lost. This way I would have some chance of retaining my job by claiming I was not around when the flag was lowered.

The manager who was actually faced with this situation knew that a nearby supplier was about to deliver some food supplies. The manager called the delivery man and told him to hurry over and knock down the flagpole with the delivery truck. The delivery man did this. The manager then phoned his boss and said the flagpole was knocked down by the delivery truck, but he would have it back up the next day. He made no mention of the fact he had the flagpole intentionally knocked down.

Exercise 9-3

This exercise is discussed in the chapter content.

Exercise 9-4

A linear solution is for the princess to choose one stone and sacrifice her happiness. Another is to expose the queen's trickery.

One of the twenty or so good divergent solutions is for the princess to ask the queen to choose a stone and then say that since the queen chose a diamond the one remaining for the princess must be a ruby.

Exercise 9-5

Sometimes men come by the name of genius in the same way that certain insects come by the name of centipede: not because they have a hundred feet, but because most people can't count above fourteen.

— *Georg Christoph Lichtenberg*

You shouldn't have to be stuck with this flag from the comic strip. Use divergent thinking and send the comic strip depicting the flag to George Bush. If he likes flags so much, he should be happy to get another one, even if it is on paper.

Exercise 9-6

Although the parking lot was intended strictly for tenants and not for hourly parkers, Barr posted several big signs advertising parking for $10.00 an hour or portion of an hour. This rate is about five to ten times the normal rate for parking in Vancouver. The outrageous rate helped curb about 75 percent of the illegal parking that occurred before the signs were posted. A little problem has arisen; occasionally, someone actually comes into the building wanting to pay the $10.00 minimum fee.

Mind Bender 1: Some solutions are one and three from 1/3, eleven (XI) and two (II) from XI/II, and four letters from thir/teen.

Mind Bender 2: The prime minister of Britain lives in the official residence at 10 Downing Street, London, S. W. 1, England, and the prime minister of Canada lives in the official residence at 24 Sussex Drive, Ottawa, K1A 0A2, Canada. Now go back and try the exercise again. (See Appendix, page 180, for the solution.)

Mind Bender 3: The man is bald.

Mind Bender 4: The farmer eats duck eggs.

Mind Bender 5: A nickel and a quarter make one of the coins not a nickel.

Mind Bender 6: Eleven (all except February).

Mind Bender 7: Male, all, mall, small can become smaller. Also pig (piglet).

Mind Bender 8: A coin marked 6 B.C. doesn't make any sense, since it means before Christ and only coins later than Christ could be marked B.C.

Mind Bender 9: The woman was born on February 29, on a leap year, and is now forty years old.

Mind Bender 10: Open all four links in one of the five chains at a cost of $4.00. Then use these to join together the remaining four chains at a cost of $6.00. Total cost is $10.00.

Rebus Mind Benders: Don't be so lazy. Show some respect and spend a little more time on these. It took me several hours to create these and you want the solutions in a minute or two! (After you have put in some more time trying to solve these, see Appendix, page 181, for the solutions.)

> The trouble with most folks ain't so much their ignorance as knowing so many things that ain't so.
>
> — *Josh Billings*

Boy, Are You Lucky You Have Problems

So What's Your Problem?

How do you view day-to-day problems? Do you always look at a big or complicated problem as an unpleasant situation? Well, you shouldn't. Creative people look at most complex problems as opportunities for growth. Each problem should be welcomed in your life as more opportunity to attain satisfaction. Our greatest satisfaction comes from solving complex problems.

Visit your mother today. Maybe she hasn't had any problems lately.

— *Graffito*

Problems offer great opportunity in our lives, if we want them to. Individuals and corporations will not only survive, but flourish in today's rapidly changing world if they are good problem solvers. Good problem solvers are those who welcome problems and are challenged by them. The challenges start their creative juices flowing. The prescription for success in the modern world is the ability to enjoy and take advantage of problems.

Exercise 10-1. As Easy as Rolling Off a Log

Assume you have a boss who isn't very good with figures. In fact, your boss is the worst person you know when it comes to math. Whenever your boss has a mathematical calculation to do, he comes

98

to see you. Today he wants you to calculate the following equation for him.

$$123 + 456 - 23 = ?$$

Undoubtedly, you had no trouble with exercise 10-1, but how much satisfaction are you experiencing from having solved this problem? Unless you are as bad at math as your fictitious boss, you likely aren't getting any satisfaction at all. Why not? Simply because there wasn't much challenge. If you had a job in which you were required to do elementary math calculations, no matter how high the pay, satisfaction attained would be nil.

Exercise 10-2. A 5,000-Year-Old Puzzle to Solve

Now let's assume that your boss also likes puzzles. He is pretty good at puzzles but is stumped by one, which he brings to you. This puzzle is about 5,000 years old and was developed by the Chinese. Can you solve it?

If:

‾ ‾
‾‾‾‾‾‾‾‾ = 6
‾‾‾‾‾‾‾‾

‾‾‾‾‾‾‾‾
‾ ‾ = 1
‾ ‾

‾‾‾‾‾‾‾‾
‾‾‾‾‾‾‾‾ = 3
‾ ‾

What Does: ‾ ‾
‾ ‾ Represent?
‾‾‾‾‾‾‾‾

> The chief cause of problems is solutions.
> — *Eric Sevareid*

If you solved both exercises, which gave you more satisfaction? Obviously, the second one did. (See Chapter Notes, page 106, for the solution to the second exercise.) This is a simple manifestation of how increasing the degree of difficulty in problem solving increases the amount of satisfaction.

The point is, The greater the challenge, the more satisfaction that is experienced from solving the problem.

My House Burned Down and Now I Can See the Moon

Being creative means welcoming problems as opportunities for attaining greater satisfaction in life. The next time you encounter a big problem at work, be conscious of your reactions. If you are self-confident, you will experience a good feeling because you have another opportunity to test your creativity. For those of you who feel anxious, remember that you have the ability to be creative and solve problems. Any problem at hand is a great opportunity to generate innovative solutions and extract satisfaction by successfully solving the problem. The Chinese have a proverb that says, "My house burned down and now I can see the moon." I certainly hope your house or anyone else's doesn't burn down. However, I hope you are able to look at some of your common and not-so-common problems and see some opportunity there.

Creativity Principle:

See Problems as Opportunities

We all have two choices when faced with problems. The first option is to resist the problem. This is somewhat ineffective. Resistance to problems stems from fear, laziness, or a lack of adequate time. Whatever the reason for the resistance, the problem won't go away. Remember the rule of psychology that states that whatever we resist will persist. This is true with problems. Resistance will ensure the perpetuation of the problem.

The second option is for us to do something about the problem. We can draw on our abilities and take control. Highly creative people actually get excited about a new problem because it means a new challenge. The new challenge eventually translates into a heightened state of satisfaction and growth. This occurs when the imminent solution is attained.

The Good, the Bad, and the Ugly of Problems

Many things have been said about problems and how we should handle them. The reality of problems can appear to range from the good to the bad to the ugly. Here are some things to think about. Whether the points are perceived as good, bad, or ugly will depend upon your interpretation.

1. **Having a lot of money will not eliminate or reduce our problems.**
   Most people won't believe this, despite all the supporting evidence.
   People want to believe there is one big money deal in life that will
   take care of all their problems. This is believing in a form of Santa
   Claus; everything is going to be great once our savior brings
   something of great value for us. Remember how false this belief
   was when we were children. Our happiness was short lived and
   our problems remained.

   There is much more evidence that money won't solve problems;
   the newspapers have thousands of stories about rich people who
   are in trouble with the law or have other major problems. A recent
   survey showed that a higher percentage of people making over
   $75,000 a year were dissatisfied with their incomes than of those
   making less than $75,000 a year. A larger percentage of the rich
   have alcohol and drug problems than the general population.

   I have a theory about how well off
   we will be with a lot of money. If we are
   happy and handle problems well when
   we are making $25,000 a year, we will be
   happy and handle problems well when
   we have a lot more money. If we are
   unhappy and don't handle problems well
   on $25,000 a year, we can expect the same
   of ourselves with a lot of money. We will
   be just as unhappy and handle problems
   as ineffectively, but with more comfort
   and style.

   I do things a little differently. For forty
   five minutes, I'll complain about my life
   so your problems won't seem so bad
   after all!

2. **Successful people in business have
   more and bigger problems to handle
   than others who are less successful.** People who have what it
   takes to make money or run a large company handle and solve
   problems well. Consequently, they are responsible for more and
   bigger problems. A recent survey in *Canadian Business* magazine
   reported that chief executive officers of Canada's largest
   corporations work an average of eleven hours a day. Evidently,
   these CEOs spend a lot of time solving many big problems.
   Millionaires claim that they still have problems, only more of
   them.

3. **Certain problems can be given away.** This is one of the most
   effective ways to solve problems. I had a problem in negotiating
   my speaking services because of the time required and because I

liked doing other tasks more. This problem is one I gave away. I now have a speaker bureau negotiating on my behalf. If you have a problem with a postal clerk who says it is impossible to send your package to a certain destination, the worst thing to do is to complain about the fact it can't be done. The clerk will become defensive, and your problem will still be there. Instead, give your problem away. Say to the clerk, "Now what would you do if you were in my shoes?" By giving your problem to the clerk, you have increased the chances that he or she will find some creative way for getting the package to its destination. If you are a manager, you can give many of your problems away. How? By delegating, of course. Think about problems you can get rid of by giving them to others. Then give them away.

> When you don't have any money, the problem is food. When you have money, it's sex. When you have both, it's health. . . . If everything is simply jake, then you're frightened of death.
>
> — *J. P. Donleavy*

4. **When we solve a problem, often it creates more problems.** This has many variations. Our problem may be that we wish to be married. Once we solve this by getting married, we then get to enjoy all the problems of marriage. Another problem may be our lack of enough clothes. Once solved, we don't have enough closet space and don't know what to wear. Not having enough money, when solved with a lottery win, leads to many other problems, such as old friends not having anything to do with us.

5. **Painful incidents or major personal setbacks are often opportunities for creative growth and transformation.** Many individuals report that going through a divorce or losing the whole wad in Las Vegas can give the mind a good rattling. The result is an experience of creative awakening. Acts of failure, such as not being promoted, can result in a rebirth of creative thinking that had remained dormant. Some people report that getting fired was the best thing that ever happened to them. Major problems are mind shakers that break old habits of thinking.

6. **A problem-free life is probably not worth living.** If we were hooked up to a machine that did everything for us, we would eliminate all of our problems. It is likely not one of us will find this as an attractive substitute to life with its inherent problems. Yet people dream of a problem-free life.

7. **If you want to get rid of your problems, just get yourself a bigger problem.** Suppose you had a problem deciding what to do this afternoon. As you were contemplating your dilemma, a big,

mean grizzly bear started chasing you. The small problem of not knowing what to do will have been eliminated by the bigger problem of the grizzly. The next time that you have a problem, create a bigger one to get rid of the first one. The smaller problem will be easily forgotten.

8. **The best way to enjoy business problems is to be doing a job or running a company we really like.** If we want to be master problem solvers, it is terribly important that we love our work. That means we should quit distasteful jobs. The best time to do it is now, and we must forget the excuses for staying in situations that we do not relish. Finding work we like means we get to handle problems that we find enjoyable to solve.

> Swallow a toad in the morning if you want to encounter nothing more disgusting the rest of the day.
> — *Nicolas Chamfort*

9. **Most problems can be transformed instantaneously just by changing the context in which we look at them.** Why is it that some person can lose all of his millions of dollars and walk away saying, "Big deal, it's only money, I still have me"? Compare this to another well-off person who gets a five-dollar parking ticket and loses sleep over it for two nights. The difference is in the context in which the two look at problems.

It isn't the reality or the degree of the problem, but the perceptual choice that determines how we view the seriousness of problems. We can change the quality of our lives just by choosing to change the context in which we view our problems. Context is about whether we see the glass is half empty or half full. Life works much better when we choose to see the glass as half full.

> If all our misfortunes were laid in one common heap whence everyone must take an equal portion, most people would be contented to take their own and depart.
> — *Socrates*

Other People's Problems Can Be Your Opportunities

People have millions of problems. These are our opportunities. The ability to spot and solve other people's problems can enrich our lives. Astute problem spotters and solvers are the movers and shakers in business.

Exercise 10-3. Focusing on Others' Problems

There is no such thing as a problem without a gift for you in its hands.

You seek problems because you need their gifts.

— *Richard Bach*

Identify five problems that others have in personal and business life. Then see if you can come up with some ideas on how to solve these problems by providing new products or services that people will buy.

People's Problems Ripe for Business Opportunities

1. People addicted to the Internet
2. Need for more freshwater
3. Too many people who feel they are victims
4. How to better utilize energy resources
5. How to have more young people working and more older people not working
6. Too many stray dogs and cats
7. How to enjoy more leisure time
8. Resorts that are not affordable
9. Schools that do not teach creative thinking
10. Businesses that want to improve productivity
11. Need for more satisfying work
12. Cheaper housing required
13. Vacant space in commercial buildings not being rented out
14. Companies that are too complicated to run
15. Many good products that aren't marketed effectively
16. More cheap day care desired
17. How to save for retirement
18. Some cities that are not friendly places
19. How to decrease illiteracy
20. Too many businesses going bankrupt
21. How to solve world hunger
22. Quality of education in schools
23. Too many young adults dropping out of schools
24. How to find missing children
25. How to be happy in retirement
26. How to reduce the divorce rate
27. Loneliness experienced by married and single individuals
28. How to prevent suicides
29. People wanting more of a sense of community in their lives
30. Not enough information
31. Too much information
32. People who do not know how to take responsibility
33. People who want to make a difference
34. How to increase one's self-esteem
35. Shoddy products
36. How to find the right job
37. How singles can meet new people
38. How to become self-actualized
39. How to spend money prudently
40. How to be happier in life
41. How to have more power
42. How to get corporate funding for community and social programs

The new year brings 365 days of opportunity.

— *Unknown Wise Person*

43. How to reduce stress at work
44. How to be healthy and look young
45. How to find a cheap vacation
46. How to avoid nagging relatives and in-laws
47. Too many choices in life
48. Insufficient time to get everything accomplished
49. How to prevent crime
50. How to enlarge this list to 100 items

Exercise 10-4. Your Own Bug List for Fun or Profit

Think about this: What bugs you? What bugs other people? Choose two "big" bugs and dream up services or products that will help eliminate these bugs.

People's Bug List

Opportunities for New Products and Services

1. Telephone solicitors
2. Having to lick envelopes and stamps
3. Too much news on the radio
4. Negative people
5. Overly positive people
6. Secondhand cigarette smoke
7. Cellular telephones ringing in restaurants
8. Not enough signs on the streets
9. Big potholes on the road
10. Having to commute too far
11. Too much traffic in neighborhood
12. Terrible books
13. Finding the right shoelaces
14. Dripping faucets
15. Collection agents
16. Having to take a car to a repair shop
17. Relatives
18. Insecure show-off yuppies
19. Burnt-out lightbulbs
20. Having to buy a Christmas tree
21. Too much negative news in newspapers
22. Autocratic bosses
23. Not knowing what to write in letters
24. Boredom with life
25. Government red tape
26. Boring speakers at conferences
27. Yappy dogs
28. Bad service in retail outlets
29. Instruction manuals too difficult to understand
30. Cars parked in front of your house
31. Dents on your car when in parking lots
32. People taking up two parking stalls
33. People who drive too slow or too fast
34. Charities that sell their mailing lists to other charities
35. Having to write an essay, article, book, resume, etc.
36. Two-for-one pizza of which even one isn't worth eating
37. Boredom on airplane flights
38. Running shoes that never feel broken in
39. One good stocking left
40. Junk mail

> I shall make electricity so cheap that only the rich can afford to burn candles.
>
> — *Thomas Edison*

41. Small bathtubs
42. Having to mow lawns
43. Noisy parties next door
44. Having to wait in lines
45. Members of the opposite sex who come on too strong

46. Too much advertising on TV and in magazines
47. Offensive TV commercials
48. Uncomfortable seats at Starbucks
49. Having to deal with obnoxious people
50. Long lists like this one

Big Problems, Big Opportunities

When it comes to problems, we must remember that the bigger the problem, the bigger the opportunity. Here is an example:

> Our disasters have been some of the best things that ever happened to us. And what we swore were blessings have been some of the worst.
>
> — *Richard Bach*

Bette Nesmith Graham had a big problem. She worked as a typist but made many typing errors. Bette knew that other typists had the same problem. Because of this, she founded a multimillion-dollar industry. In the early fifties, IBM introduced their new electric typewriters with carbon film ribbons. When typists tried to erase typographical errors, a terrible mess was left behind on the paper. To overcome this problem, Bette developed a white paint to use in correcting her typos. The paint worked well. She called it Liquid Paper. When Bette Graham offered IBM her new product, she was turned down. This problem was also an opportunity. She decided to market Liquid Paper herself. When Bette died in 1980, she was worth 50 million dollars.

Our careers or businesses depend on individuals' problems. All of our work involves some sort of problem solving. People will always have problems; we will always have many opportunities for solving these problems. Focusing on problems can make us rich and famous (if that is what we want). Even more important than wealth and fame are the satisfaction and enjoyment that come from effective solving of problems.

Chapter Notes

Exercise 10-2

The answer is four. By looking at the first three sets of three lines we can determine a pattern. The first line of the three represents one, the second represents two, and the third represents four. If any of these lines is broken, then the line represents zero. The sum of the three lines represents the number. Therefore, the one in question is the following:

$$0 + 0 + 4 = 4$$

How to Be a Successful Failure

To Be More Successful, Fail a Lot More

Exercise 11-1. Name This Man

Twice this person failed in business. He ran for state legislature and didn't make it. Two times he lost in his bid for Congress. He did no better in the Senate races; twice he was defeated. Success eluded him when he worked hard to become vice president of the United States. The woman he loved died when she was very young. Eventually, this man suffered a nervous breakdown.

Who was this man?

> All profoundly original art looks ugly at first.
>
> — *Clement Greenberg*

Exercise 11-2. The Key to Business Success

What is the most important quality, above all else, that chief executives and entrepreneurs have that helps them achieve their success?

The last chapter stressed that problems are opportunities and the bigger the problem to solve, the greater satisfaction we will obtain from solving that problem. If this is the case, why do many people avoid certain problems more than they would avoid a pit bull terrier with rabies? One of the biggest reasons is fear of failure.

Many people avoid the risk of failure, not realizing that success usually comes after a lot of failure. Take the example of the man in exercise 11-1. This man was none other than Abraham Lincoln. All his "failure" happened before he became one of the most famous presidents of the United States.

On one hand, North American society is obsessed with attaining success. On the other hand, most people are afraid of failure and try to avoid it. The need for success and the desire to avoid failure are contradictory. Failure is just a necessary step to success. Often you will have to experience many failures before you experience success. The road to success looks something like this:

Failure Failure Failure Failure Failure Failure
Failure Failure Failure Success

> A lot of disappointed people have been left standing on the street corner waiting for the bus marked Perfection.
>
> — *Donald Kennedy*

The road to success is paved with failure — failure and nothing else. Yet many people attempt to avoid failure at all costs. Fear of failure is associated with other fears, such as fear of being seen as a fool, fear of being criticized, fear of losing the respect of the group, and fear of losing financial security. Avoiding failure means avoiding success. You have to fail a lot to attain success. Of course, the way to double your success rate is to double your failure rate.

Fear of Being a Fool Is Foolish

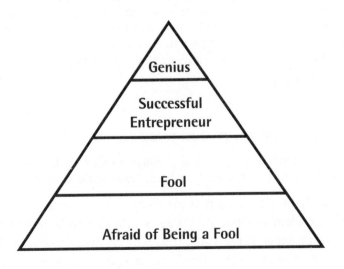

Participants in my seminars cite the fear of failure as a creativity barrier or bandit; however, I point out to them that it isn't the fear of failure but the fear of what others will think about us. Many of us avoid taking risks because we are afraid to look bad if we fail. We get so obsessed with being liked that we won't do things that we feel may make us look bad in the eyes of others. Avoidance of risk becomes the norm. This is detrimental not only to our creativity but to our liveliness as well. We must learn to be fools if we are to be creative and live life to the fullest.

Creativity Principle:

Take Risks

Many of us believe there is a hierarchy in life as shown above. On top are the geniuses. Then come the successful entrepreneurs, who never fail. If we take a hard look at the apparent geniuses of the world, we find that genius is nothing more than perseverance and persistence disguised. Einstein and Edison had many successes, but they also had an incredible number of failures.

There is level worse than being a fool: "Afraid of being a fool" is much worse than being a fool. Geniuses, effective leaders, and successful entrepreneurs have handled the fear of being a fool. They realize that in order to succeed in their endeavors they have to first be a fool; being foolish is essential to life's mastery. Being "a fool" is on a much higher plane than being "afraid of being a fool." Life requires that we be fools now and then.

> There is a thin line between genius and insanity. I have erased that line.
>
> — *Oscar Levant*

If you worry a lot about what others will think about you, I have some important news for you: Researchers indicate that on a good day 80 percent of all individuals' thoughts are negative. Just think what percentage this is on a bad day. It looks like most people are going to have bad thoughts about you anyway. That is what most individuals' thinking is all about. So what difference does it make? The heck with what others think! You may as well go for it!

Try Celebrating Your Failures

Successful entrepreneurs and managers are good at taking risks. Seldom do they take outrageous risks. The risks they take are normally calculated to be reasonable, so the chances of winning are not so small as to be a stupid gamble and not so large as to be a sure thing. Today's leaders give themselves challenges that represent a reasonable probability of loss and a reasonable probability of gain.

Let's return to exercise 11-2. There are many important factors for the success of entrepreneurs and managers. These include communication, vision, leadership, integrity, sensitivity, flexibility in thinking, confidence, courage, and constructive nonconformity. But the Center for Creative Leadership in Greensboro, North Carolina, found one factor that stands out more than the others. This is what gives achievers the final edge.

The biggest factor is their ability to manage failure. Successful people aren't hindered or stopped by failure. They look at failure differently. They learn from it; they actually welcome and celebrate failure.

My mom says we learn something from every one of our mistakes. I'm not sure my brain is big enough to hold that much learning."

Setbacks Experienced by Successful People

With risk comes the probability of failure. That's the price we must be prepared to accept. The greater the risks, the greater the probability of loss. However, with greater risks come bigger payoffs. Here are some examples of people who have succeeded despite their initial failures in life.

- Diane Sawyer has had one of the best jobs in television news as the network newscaster for *Prime Time Live*. Sawyer paid her dues working as a weather reporter in Louisville, Kentucky, for three years.

- Actor (and comedian) Robin Williams was voted least likely to succeed by his classmates.

- Before Christie Brinkley became a supermodel, she had a tendency to be overweight and admitted she was "a self-conscious teenager who was chubby with chipmunk cheeks."

- Jay Leno, host of the *Tonight Show*, once worked as an opening act in a brothel.

- A teacher described one of his young students as "mentally slow, unsociable — adrift in his foolish dreams." The young student was Albert Einstein, who could not speak until he was four years old and didn't read until he was seven.

- John Grisham, author of *The Firm* and *The Client,* which have sold millions of copies, had his first novel *(A Time to Kill)* rejected by twenty-eight publishers. When Wynwood Press undertook *A Time to Kill,* it sold only 5,000 copies.

- Michael Jordan didn't make his high school basketball team in his second year because the coach said he wasn't good enough.

> The worst part of success is trying to find someone who is happy for you.
> — *Bette Midler*

- Television personality Phil Donahue starting working in a bank after he failed his first audition as a radio broadcaster.

- Matthew Coon Come, grand chief of the Quebec Cree Indians, has had many setbacks battling Hydro-Quebec, trying to protect his people's land from flooding and river diversions. However, through his creative ways of bringing attention to this matter and his victories in Canadian courts, he has prompted the cancellation of lucrative Hydro-Quebec export contracts. Recently, Coon Come won one of the world's prestigious environmental awards, the $60,000 prize from the Goldman Environmental Foundation.

- Jane Pauley became a winner as a famous television personality on *Dateline NBC* but she was a six-time loser in the homecoming queen elections at her school.

Exercise 11–3. What do these people have in common?

- Lee Iaccoca (former CEO of Chrysler)
- Sally Jessy Raphael (television talk-show host)
- Rush Limbaugh (radio talk-show host)
- Lily Tomlin (actress and comedian)
- David Letterman (television talk-show host)
- Stephen Jobs (founder of Apple Computer, Inc.)
- Ernie Zelinski

> To rebel in season is not to rebel.
> — *Greek Proverb*

I bet most of you wanted to say that what all the above people have in common is they're all famous; however, my name on the list destroyed that thought. Actually, the answer is all the above people were fired from their jobs at one time or another.

Lee Iaccoca was fired from Ford Motor Company, despite his great accomplishments there, before he was hired by Chrysler. Henry Ford III told Iaccoca he was being fired simply because Ford didn't like Iaccoca.

Rush Limbaugh, the popular radio broadcaster, claims he was fired from all but two of the jobs he ever had. Stephen Jobs was fired from Apple Computers, the company he cofounded. Sally Jessy Raphael was fired eighteen times in thirty-six years in the broadcasting business.

> Someone who tries to do something and fails is a lot better off than the person who tries to do nothing and succeeds.
>
> — Unknown Wise Person

David Letterman was fired from a job as a weatherman on an Indianapolis TV station for jokingly reporting hailstones the size of "canned hams." Lily Tomlin was fired from a Howard Johnson's restaurant for announcing on the PA system, "Your favorite waitress, Lily Tomlin, is about to make her appearance on the floor. Let's give her a big hand." Customers were amused but not management.

Why was I fired? At the utility company where I had worked six years, I took eight weeks of deserved vacation that my superiors didn't want me to take. I enjoyed the vacation, but the management didn't. I was given a permanent vacation when I returned to work. But I am in pretty good company, with Limbaugh, Raphael, Iaccoca, Tomlin, Jobs, and Letterman. Can you say this? If you haven't been fired from a job, you aren't being overly creative.

Warning: Success Often Leads to Failure

"Positive thinkers" want us to believe that success almost always leads to more success. There is some truth to the idea that success helps create more success. It builds confidence in individuals and organizations. In addition, many new techniques and principles are learned on the way to success. These usually help attain future success.

What "positive thinkers" often don't point out is nothing breeds failure like success. More often than is acknowledged, success leads to failure. There are two major reasons for this. The first one is the law of averages. Normally, we have more unsuccessful endeavors than successful ones. The odds for failure are much greater than for success, even just after being successful.

The second reason for success leading to failure relates to ego and complacency. Organizations and individuals who make it big usually get fat heads. They tend to think they have the solution and now know it all. Nothing can be further from the truth. No matter how successful a product, service, or technique is, it won't be the right one for all circumstances. As we know, circumstances have a tendency to change. When circumstances change abruptly, many organizations and individuals are faced with a product, service, or technique that no longer serves its purpose well. The organization or individual isn't able to adequately respond to the new business climate. Tough times follow.

Entrepreneurs have been known to build highly successful companies and then find themselves in deep financial trouble. What sometimes happens is, entrepreneurs, men more so than women, want to show the world they have arrived. They buy big houses, expensive cars, and a host of other items. Money is siphoned out of the business just when the business becomes highly successful. Competitors usually move in when they see a business making it big in a certain industry. This is when the successful business requires a large amount of money to deal with the competition. If it doesn't have the money, the once successful company soon finds itself in deep financial trouble. Success then leads to failure.

What a Difference Being Different Makes!

Exercise 11–4. A Common Trait in Uncommon People

What did the following people have in common?

- Mother Teresa
- Thomas Edison
- Albert Einstein
- John F. Kennedy
- Gandhi

Creativity Principle:

Dare to Be Different

What is the best way to make a big difference in this world? Answer: *Start off by being different.* Being creative is thinking something different. It is also being different than most people. We must diverge from the norm to generate something new and worthwhile. This will take courage, since people who diverge from the norm are frowned upon. We must dare to be different if we are to achieve something important.

If you want your life to be interesting and exciting, be different. Be different than you normally are and be different than the majority of people in your life. One warning must be given here. You won't get much support from your friends, co-workers, or society when you take the step to be different. They certainly won't encourage you to stand out.

Your motivation to be different has to come from within. The motivation should come from the realization that anything of major consequence in this world was probably initiated by someone who was different than the rest of society. In fact they were probably out of step with society to a large degree.

Just think about the individuals in exercise 11-4. Thomas Edison, Albert Einstein, Mother Teresa, Gandhi, and John F. Kennedy made a big difference. What they have in common is that they were different than the majority. They were out of step; none of these people were conformists.

Two roads diverged in a wood, and I took the one less travelled by, And that has made all the difference.

— Robert Frost

The point is that being an achiever means being different and feeling good about it. Some people may be uncomfortable with you, and others may dislike you for it. You will be criticized a lot. The more success you have at being different, the more you may be disliked. But people will respect you for it, especially when you start making that big difference. You will also have your own respect.

Society's norms often dictate how we act and the goals we pursue. We think that to feel good about ourselves, we must be liked by everyone, or at least as many people as possible. Indeed, just to belong to a group, we end up doing things that aren't in touch with our inner selves. This is when we lose the sense of who we really are.

There is no question that not conforming and not fitting in are often uncomfortable. You have to confront the discomfort of people jeering and criticizing you. The long-term payoff is you gain self-respect and satisfaction. Other highly motivated people will end up admiring and congratulating you for having the fortitude to stand apart from the boring crowd.

If you run, you might lose. If you don't run, you're guaranteed to lose.

— Jesse L. Jackson

Don't let the urge to be nice to everyone interfere with your being different. Having the urge to be nice to everyone translates into wanting to be liked by everyone. Robin Chandler, a British actor, states, "The disease of niceness cripples more lives than alcoholism. Nice people are simply afraid to say no, are constantly worrying about what others think of them, constantly adapting their behavior to please — never getting to do what they want to do."

Also, don't fit in just to be liked and accepted by the group. Insist on being an individual who has something unique to offer to anyone who likes individuals, and not clones. Going against the status quo and removing yourself from the herd give you a sense of who you really are. Being different means not doing something simply because everyone else is doing it. When someone suggests that you should do something because "everyone else is doing it," stop and think about the absurdity of this statement. When we are doing something because everyone else is doing it, we are being influenced by the herd instinct.

It is easy to follow the herd. You may have noticed that people in the mainstream don't fare very well in the long run. People who make a difference in any industry or field of endeavor are invariably different. Here are four more examples of people who have made a big difference by being different:

- Anita Roddick
- Margaret Thatcher
- Nelson Mandela
- Richard Branson

> Don't play for safety. It's the most dangerous game in the world.
> — *Sir Hugh Walpole*

Anita Roddick, first mentioned in chapter 6, is different because she has been known to break many rules in running her chain of stores. The Body Shop doesn't spend money on advertising in an industry that spends hundreds of millions on marketing and advertising. The Body Shop relies strictly on word of mouth. The Body Shop doesn't spend much money on research, as do most cosmetic companies. What is the main tool for its research? Nothing more than a suggestion box for customers placed in each store. In the cosmetics industry, packaging and image are important, or so say the experts. The Body Shop uses refillable bottles initially designed for a somewhat different purpose — collecting urine specimens. Roddick encourages each store to commit 25 percent (not .25 percent like many companies) of its profits to a community project. Postcards are used to print their annual reports.

Margaret Thatcher was the longest sitting British prime minister this century. It is interesting to note that Margaret Thatcher was chosen second behind Adolf Hitler as the person, past or present, most hated in a 1988 poll conducted by Madame Tussaud's Waxworks Museum in London, England. In 1983 she was chosen fourth, and in 1978 she was chosen third. She was hated, but she was respected. She was liked as well; she had to be to get elected in three consecutive elections.

> We forfeit three-fourths of ourselves to be like other people.
> — *Arthur Schopenhauer*

In 1994 Nelson Mandela became South Africa's first black president after successfully attaining his goal of eliminating apartheid in his country. In the 1960s, he was convicted of sabotage and treason during his fight against apartheid. After spending twenty-seven years in jail, he was freed. Mandela's willingness to pay the price for being different led the way for his remarkable ascent to power.

Richard Branson is dismissed by British businessmen as a "flake." Over the last few years, they have tried to discredit Branson at every turn. Branson's Virgin Atlantic Airways, against which British Airways conducted an unsuccessful smear campaign, captured $750 million in revenue in the British market. His airline stands for youth, independence, and cheekiness — also the traits of his favorite character, Peter Pan.

Richard Branson is definitely different, but highly successful and admired by the British public. BBC Radio conducted a poll to find out who should be charged with rewriting the Ten Commandments. Branson came in at fourth place after Mother Teresa, the pope, and the archbishop of Canterbury. Without question, all the businessmen who call Branson a flake would give their left arms to have the popularity and respect Branson has with the British public.

Note that if you want to attain even a sliver of the public recognition that Branson has attained, you aren't going to attain any fame in life by trying to fit in with the rest of the pack. I personally have received a modest amount of publicity with well over 100 newspaper articles, national TV interviews, radio talk-show appearances, and magazine features about my books and lifestyle. This free publicity probably would have cost me in the neighborhood of $200,000 if I had to buy equivalent advertising space for my books. Of course, paid advertising wouldn't have been as credible and effective. The point is, this valuable publicity wasn't a result of my trying to fit in with the rest of the pack.

Creativity varies inversely with the number of cooks involved in the broth.

— Bernice Fitz-Gibbon

Just getting your fifteen minutes of fame, as promised by Andy Warhol, will be extremely difficult if you are a carbon copy of everyone else. The news media isn't in the business of gratuitously writing about just anyone. The news media is in the business of providing interesting stories for its readers. I found out long ago that the chances for the news media writing about me are increased dramatically if I follow these three principles:

- Be first.
- Be different.
- Be daring.

Being first is important. If I asked you which team was second to climb Mount Everest, you probably wouldn't know and would reply, "Who cares?" In most cases people won't remember who was second in accomplishing something important. (If you really care, the second team to reach the top of Mount Everest was Jurg Marmet and Ernest Schmidt.)

Being different and daring are important as well. Dick Drew, host of the national network radio program called *The Canadian Achievers* and author of the book with the same name, has the following quotation printed on his business card. I have found the quotation to be empowering and carry Drew's business card with me so that I can read the quotation from time to time.

> When one jumps over the edge, one is bound to land somewhere.
>
> — *D. H. Lawrence*

If you follow the crowd, you will likely get no further than the crowd. If you walk alone, you're likely to end up in places no one has ever been before.

Being an achiever is not without its difficulties, for peculiarity breeds contempt. The unfortunate thing about being ahead of your time is that when people finally realize you were right, they'll simply say it was obvious to everyone all along.

You have two choices in life. You can dissolve into the mainstream, or you can choose to become an achiever and be distinct. To be distinct, you must be different. To be different, you must strive to be what no else but you can be.

If you want to lead an anonymous life, then go ahead and be like everyone else — fit in and be part of the pack. Conforming to society, and thinking like the rest of the herd, is just another case of doing the easy thing for short-term comfort. When you do this, there is nothing unique about you. You get to fit in and be liked a little bit by everyone. However, in the long term, life is difficult because your self-respect suffers, and there is no satisfaction from having accomplished something significantly different.

> Where all men think alike, no one thinks very much.
>
> — *Walter Lippmann*

Trying to fit in because you want to be liked by everyone may result in your getting liked just a little bit by most people, but not liked a lot by anyone. You will certainly never attain great recognition or any fame by following the herd. You are unique and deserve unique treatment, so don't try to be the same as everyone else.

For Happiness and Longevity, Try Eccentricity

Alan Fairweather of Scotland eats only potatoes, either baked, boiled, or fried. On the rare occasion, he may break this rule and eat a chocolate bar to add variety to his life. Fairweather not only chooses potatoes as the mainstay in his diet — he makes potatoes his life. He works as a potato inspector for the Agricultural Ministry in Scotland. Needless to say, Fairweather loves potatoes.

You are probably thinking, "Fairweather is an eccentric." You are absolutely right. Whatever else you are thinking, don't feel sorry for Fairweather and others like him. Fairweather is a "true" eccentric, according to psychologist Dr. David Weeks and writer Jamie James, who both wrote the book *Eccentrics*.

Eccentrics, like potato-lover Fairweather, spend a great deal of time alone; however, Weeks and James found that eccentrics are certainly not unhappy people. Quite surprisingly, Weeks and James found that eccentrics are much happier than the rest of the population. They are also healthier and tend to live much longer. And for those of you who think people like Fairweather are crazy, Weeks and James concluded that eccentrics are much more intelligent than the general population. True eccentrics are nonconforming, highly creative, curious, idealistic, intelligent, opinionated, and obsessed with some hobby. Weeks and James studied over 900 eccentrics and found that the majority of these men and women live alone because others find them too peculiar to live with. Nonetheless, spending time alone is not a problem for true eccentrics; they thrive on it.

Eccentrics have a lot of freedom, a luxury that many people don't allow themselves. They are free to pursue hobbies and lifestyles that are their passions. Freed from the need to conform, eccentrics aren't bothered by what others think of them. Their important traits, especially self-confidence and a sense of freedom, help them achieve great happiness and longevity. So, the moral of the story is, for happiness and longevity, try eccentricity.

Rules and Assumptions Not to Be Ruled By

Being different means challenging the status quo. It is a good idea for individuals and organizations to constantly challenge rules and assumptions. Discarding outmoded rules and unproven assumptions throws a new perspective on business situations. Innovation tends to flow freer and the performance of organizations improves.

Many rules, both written and unwritten, are outdated and serve absolutely no purpose. Often, rules are followed without any thought to whether there is a purpose for them. Rules can hinder the generation of new ideas and impede implementation of innovative ways of doing business.

For many years Canadian doctors and lawyers subjected themselves to a rule that restricted the advertising of their services. This rule interfered with their ability to tell the public about their business and the types of services they had to offer. Only after constant challenging of this rule by their members have these professionals come to grips with the obsolescence of the rule. Now more advertising is allowed.

Creativity Principle:

Challenge Rules and Assumptions

We should constantly challenge not only rules but also assumptions. Our voices of judgment constantly make assumptions about the way things are. Often these assumptions have little or no relationship to the ways things are. Only through challenging assumptions can we determine their validity.

For example, most managers still erroneously assume money is the prime motivator of employees. If managers make the wrong assumption that all employees are motivated by money, they will be ineffective in motivating employees. Researchers have found that recognition and room for growth are better motivators than money. Money as the prime motivator is only one of many wrong assumptions being made that hinder organizational effectiveness.

Breaking the Rules for Fun and Profit

Many businesses owe their success to their willingness to challenge prevailing assumptions and rules of their industry. Because most businesses don't have the presence of mind to challenge the status quo, a great deal of opportunity exists for the businesses and individuals who develop new methods by challenging the rules. If we look at any of today's highly successful businesses, we will see businesses that are risking, being different, and challenging the rules.

Following are two examples of individuals with businesses who have profited from their willingness to challenge old ways of doing business.

- Steven Nichols went in the opposite direction and broke the rules by which Nike and Reebok play in the multimillion-dollar sneaker business. For the big companies the average shelf life for sneaker models is four months. These companies base sales strategy on having ever-changing trendy models for fickle teenagers. Nichols with his K-Swiss Company has taken his sales from $20 million in 1986 to $150 million in 1993 by selling models that aren't discontinued to a more mature market of weekend athletes and tennis enthusiasts. Many retailers

> There ain't no rules around here! We're trying to accomplish something!
> — *Thomas Edison*

like his sneakers because they don't have to constantly discount discontinued models and replace them with trendy models.

- To differentiate his company's cough syrup from the competition, Frank Buckley decided to risk and break a rule of advertising that states you should not focus on the negatives of your product. W.K. Buckley Ltd.'s cough mixture was invented seventy years ago. It tasted awful at the time and still tastes awful. In the mid-1980s, Buckley's Mixture sales had fallen to 4 percent of market share for cough syrups. Defying conventional marketing wisdom, Frank Buckley decided to emphasize Buckley's Mixture's bad taste in the product's promotional campaign. For example, a transit ad featured Frank Buckley's sour face, with the ad copy, "I wake up with nightmares that someone is giving me a taste of my own medicine." Buckley's advertising campaign's won several awards. The cough mixture's sales increased 16 percent in 1989, when industry sales declined 1 percent and market share rose to 6 percent.

> Creativity comes by breaking the rules, by saying you're in love with the anarchist.
> — *Anita Roddick*

Ya Gotta Break the Rules When Ya Speak

The presenter paced frantically. He put his hands in his pockets. He yelled. He swore. He didn't dress as well as he could have. I discussed this speaker's performance with the 1989–1990 International President of Toastmasters. He observed that this speaker broke every rule of Toastmasters except one. The rule this speaker didn't break: Connect with your audience.

Whether you are a university student or a chief executive officer, you will probably have to make a presentation before a group at one time or another. My advice is, if you want to make an effective speech, learn the rules of speaking, and then break as many of them as you can.

The speaker cited above was Tom Peters, coauthor of *In Search of Excellence* and several other best-selling books. He didn't follow the rules, yet he drew over 1,500 people to his Vancouver performance. His annual income from speaking engagements reportedly runs into the millions.

> When both a speaker and an audience are confused, the speech is profound.
> — *Oscar Wilde*

One reason Tom Peters does so well is he is a creative person. Being creative in any endeavor means challenging and sometimes breaking both written and unwritten rules. Rules relate to process and we often concentrate too much on following the right process instead of getting the right results.

Anyone who has read a book or taken a course on how to make effective presentations has encountered many rules for doing things right. A lot of these are perfectly valid — as guidelines. Taken as commandments, they can actually hurt your performance.

Here are seven rules commonly propounded by people who specialize in teaching us how to make good presentations. Some I break regularly myself without anyone seeming to suffer. The rest I have seen other speakers break to their advantage.

> Most people can tire of a lecture in ten minutes; clever people can do it in five. Sensible people never go to lectures at all.
>
> — *Stephen Leacock*

Rule — Know Exactly What You Are Going to Say. It is important to have a basic plan for any speech or presentation. But sticking entirely to your planned presentation can rob you of the opportunity to discover something new. In seminars and university lectures, I often leave open a section of my presentation for "winging it." Some of the most valuable planned activities I now use were discovered spontaneously when I tried something new.

Rule — Take a Break After an Hour. Ninety minutes into a recent three-hour presentation on creativity, I asked the participants if they wanted a break. They suggested that we continue and take our coffee on the run. We never did take an official break during that session, and the ratings were excellent — so much for the rule about the break. The point is that if you have generated a high energy level, you don't have to kill the momentum halfway through the presentation because the clock strikes 10:00 A.M. Breaks are for the participants' benefit; take one when it will benefit the participants.

Rule — Allow Discussion But Not Arguments. The purpose of this rule apparently is to eliminate unpleasantness. Yes, heated debates are distasteful to some people, but others enjoy them. "I like sessions which get my adrenaline flowing" read the comment on the seminar evaluation form that first prompted me to start breaking the "no arguments" rule. I now encourage heated debates. More people appear to enjoy this than be put off by it. Yes, vigorous arguments have to be managed properly, but they can make a session far more engaging to most participants.

Rule — Allow Time for Questions. This indeed may be an ironclad rule if you're responsible for training people. But if you're essentially just delivering a speech? A few of the best-paid speakers admit that they avoid questions because they aren't good at answering them. Avoiding questions doesn't seem to hurt them. These speakers remain highly popular; they get hired again and again. If you want to avoid questions, see if you can get away with it. If your audience likes your presentation, you will have no problem.

Rule — Use Visuals. At an international conference a few months ago, an expert on critical thinking spoke for one and a half hours without using a single visual aid. His presentation was one of the best I have ever heard. I also saw a presenter who didn't move from the overhead projector for his entire ninety-minute presentation. If not awful, he was mediocre at best. A lot of speakers (I am one of them) make a rule always to use some visuals. I don't believe everyone has to.

Rule — Don't Get Upset, and If You Do, Don't Show It. The North American advice industry possesses a somewhat peculiar belief there is something intrinsically wrong with a speaker getting angry or highly emotional. I do not share this belief. If I have a good reason, I don't hold back. I let the audience know I how I feel. What benefit can result from being emotional in front of people? Getting upset shows the participants that I care. If I care, they care as well.

He charged nothing for his preaching and it was worth it too.

— *Mark Twain*

Rule — Don't Make Fun of Anyone. I can make fun of certain characters and have everyone in the session happy. When someone obviously is looking for attention in my sessions, I pick on this person. To this type of character, negative attention is better than none at all. The person is happy to get the attention. The rest of the participants are happy to see me pick on the "jerk." Of course, I am happy to have all the participants happy. Note that you shouldn't poke fun at just anyone for the sake of ridicule alone.

As a public speaker, the only rule you shouldn't break is to connect with your audience. If you're doing everything else by the book, but failing to connect, it's time you threw away the rule book. Try breaking some of those rules for a change.

Creative Thinking Is an Exercise In Silliness

Kilroy was not here!
— Clem

Growing Up May Be Harmful to Your Health

The above figure is one of the mysterious "Clem," who originated in Britain and has appeared in thousands of washrooms across many nations. He has been mistaken for the legendary "Kilroy was here," which originated in United States and has also had great washroom presence. Over the years Kilroy's name has been combined with Clem's picture in North American washrooms. Most North Americans think Clem is Kilroy. Not so. Clem is Clem and Kilroy is Kilroy.

> Imagination was given to man to compensate him for what he is not. A sense of humor was provided to console him for what he is.
>
> — *Horace Walpole*

By now you are probably wondering what this story has to do with this book. Absolutely nothing. I just kind of like the story and I needed a creative way to get your attention for this section. I thought this would be a good time to be silly and unreasonable. Besides, I always wanted to tell people this trivia about Clem and Kilroy, which is of absolutely no use to anyone.

Oscar Wilde said, "Life is much too important to be taken seriously." How serious are you in life? Do you find time to laugh, play, and be foolish? If you are always serious and trying to be reasonable, you are sabotaging your creativity. Individuals who are too serious to have fun rarely come up with something new and stunning.

> Look for the ridiculous in everything and you will find it.
> — *Jules Renard*

Play is at the heart of creativity. Playing and having fun are great ways to stimulate our minds. When we are having fun, we tend to be relaxed and enthusiastic. Sometimes we even let go and become outrageous. All of these states complement the creative spirit.

Hundreds of thousands of people in their sixties, seventies, eighties, and nineties have an incredible zest for life and show great vigor, enthusiasm, and physical ability in living. To some seniors, being over the hill means picking up speed. Seniors who live life to the fullest have an enlightened awareness about how alive they really are. They have developed certain character traits that really stand out.

One of the most precious traits that seniors with a zest for life have is their continuing wonder with life — the ability to enjoy each new rainbow, sunset, and full moon. Here are some other qualities that participants in my seminars list for the vibrant seniors they know:

Independent	Energetic
Diverse interests	Friendly
Creative	Inquisitive
Spontaneous	Crazy or ability to act foolish
Sense of humor	Adventurous
Playful	Joyful

Note that, whereas the above traits are manifested in a minority of the seniors' age group, these same traits are also possessed by virtually everyone in another age group: children. In other words, people who are active and happy in their later years don't need a second childhood because they never gave up their first.

Ever wonder why children are so creative? One of the important reasons is they know how to play and have fun. Remember when you were a child. When you were playing, you were learning. You probably learned a lot more during your lighter moments than during your serious moments. Try to reexperience the child in you if you want to increase your creativity.

Creativity requires playfulness, daydreaming, and foolishness — things society discourages. We are told to "grow up." We must be able to ignore what the majority in society wants. To be more creative, we must learn new ways of playing with things, words, puzzles, ideas, and people. We must never grow up. Why? When we grow up, we stop growing.

Humor Is No Laughing Matter

In his early nineties George Burns started taking bookings for his 100th birthday. Burns lived for more than a century largely because of his positive attitude, which he carried throughout his life. He made a living out of humor. Undoubtedly, his health benefited from his work. Researchers are finding that boisterous laughing many times a day will give you the same effects as a ten-mile run. Various other studies have confirmed that laughter and humor are beneficial for adjusting to major life stresses.

Creativity Principle:

Have Fun and Be Foolish

Besides being good for our health, humor is an effective way to incite creativity. Experts in creativity have observed that stunning solutions are often triggered by humor. Seriousness hinders the creative flow. When you are under a lot of stress or stuck in a serious state of mind, the best thing is to get out a joke book. Get together with someone who can laugh about anything. Fool around. You'll be surprised at the number of creative ideas that start to flow.

Several years ago a group of high-school students were given a test in creativity. Two equal groups were formed. One of the groups enjoyed the half hour before the test by listening to a recording of a comedian. The other group spent the half hour in silence. When subjected to the test, the students in the first group did much better than the second group.

Comedy and laughing will open up your thinking. Laughing tends to make you look at things in unusual ways. This is because laughter changes your state of mind. There is little concern for being wrong or being practical. It is okay to be foolish. This fosters the flow of creative solutions.

Poking fun at work situations is one way to stimulate creativity. You are more apt to break the rules when poking fun at a problem. In a state

FRANK AND ERNEST

DID I EVER TELL YOU THE STATE DEPARTMENT ONCE SENT ME TO THE FAR EAST? .. BUT I BECAME DISORIENTED, SO I JOINED A COMPANY THAT WAS LATER ABSORBED BY ACME PAPER TOWELS.

I FINALLY BECAME AN IMPORTANT EXECUTIVE IN A LARGE CORPORATION. AND THEN SOMEONE SPILLED WHITE-OUT ON THE ORGANIZATION CHART AND WIPED OUT MY WHOLE DEPARTMENT!

THAT'S THE TROUBLE WITH TODAY'S WORLD, ERNIE .. NOBODY APPRECIATES SOPHISTICATED HUMOR ANYMORE!

THAVES

© 1988 Thaves / Used with permission. Newspaper dist. by NEA, Inc.

of playing with the problem your defenses are down and your mental locks released. This results in more innovative and exciting responses to the problem at hand. Managers should learn how to encourage their employees to poke fun at all important matters in the workplace.

Exercise 12-1. Abbreviations to Elongate Your Mind

Why not have some fun before your next important office meeting? Fun puts everyone in a better state of mind. One way is to play some game or do puzzles. The abbreviations below stand for relationships and associations of which you should be aware. Have fun with these before you make up your own. Then give them to your colleagues to figure out before your next meeting.

A light heart lives long.

— *William Shakespeare*

Examples:

24H = 1D (24 Hours = 1 Day) NN = GN (No News = Good News)

1. 4 P = E
2. BMW + MB + P + J = FC
3. 12 I = 1 F
4. S + W + E + N = 4 D
5. SC resides at the NP
6. 50 S = USA
7. 10 D = 1 C
8. 1 + 3 Z = 1 T
9. LA + SF + SD are in C
10. JFK + RN + RR were P

11. IWTHYH was sung by the B
12. A PS = a PE
13. WGUMCD
14. 1 Y + 1 D = 11 Y
15. MJ sings with the RS
16. H + W + C = F
17. JC was born on CD
18. IC, IS, IC

He who laughs, lasts!
— Mary Pettibone Poole

19. S + 2 D = M
20. WP + NYT + WSJ + UST = N
21. J + P + R + G = TB
22. a LY + 4 Y = a LY
23. EJ + RS + M + MJ = S
24. CP + JFKIA are in NY
25. 24 M = 2 Y

(See Appendix, page 181, for solution to 1 and hints to the others.)

More Graffiti to Cleanse Your Mind

With all the barriers to creativity in our society, many people find that the only place they get to be creative is in the washroom. A lot of the graffiti they write is highly creative. Here are two more pages of it. Please share these with your fellow workers before your next meeting. Your group's creativity may be opened up.

GOD IS DEaD.
(Our God is alive; sorry to hear about yours.)

58 PERCENT OF ALL DEATHS ARE FATAL.

There is a dance in this town every Saturday night this week.

What will you do when Jesus comes?
(Move Gretzky to right wing.)

THERE IS NO SUCH THING AS GRAVITY. THE EARTH SUCKS.

Lassie kills chickens.

JESUS SAVES!
EVEN MORE THAN THE SUPERSTORE?

Mary had a little lamb, and boy, was she surprised.

I bet you I could stop gambling.

Dionne Quintuplets were a hoax. Five couples were charged in the conspiracy.

An empty taxi stopped and Ronald Reagan got out.

ORVILLE WAS WRIGHT.

I'm not prejudiced. I hate everyone equally.

TIME IS NATURE'S WAY OF KEEPING EVERYTHING FROM HAPPENING AT ONCE.

Can a blue man sing the whites?

The hangman lets us down.

My inferiority complexes are not as good as yours.

I wrote on this wall because it was here.

Twiggy is only skin deep.

Alimony is like buying hay for a dead cow.

Mona Lisa was framed.

CHICKEN MAN HAS A FOWL MOUTH.

If you do it in an MG, don't boast about your Triumphs.

You're never alone with schizophrenia.

Roget's Thesaurus dominates, regulates, rules, OK, all right, adequately.

GOD LOVES YOU

(God won't love you for destroying someone's property by writing on it.)

Schizophrenia Rules, OK OK!

Horse Power Rules, Neigh, Neigh

Dyslexia lures, KO

WET PAINT
(This is not an instruction.)

Hypochondria is the one disease that I don't have.

I love grils.
(which was corrected thus:)

You mean girls stupid!
(but then corrected again)

What about us grils?

ARRANGE THE FOLLOWING WORDS INTO A WELL-
KNOWN PHRASE OR SAYING:
OFF PISS

I NEVER USED TO BE ABLE TO FINISH ANYTHING, BUT NOW I.......

This wall will shortly be available in paperback.

Clairvoyance Is Dead.

I knew you were going to write this.

Absolute zero is cool.

Repeal the banana.

Kilroy Was Here! I was not.
— signed Kilroy

> If an idea does not
> appear bizarre, there
> is no hope for it.
> — *Niels Bohr*

Putting Humor to Serious Use

Here is an example of how humor helped me market my books and seminars. After publishing my first book, I wound up with about twenty-five defective books, which were either cut crooked or had missing pages. I took these back to my printer, expecting a refund. However, the printer told me he had given me eighty extra copies over and above those I paid for. Since I didn't want to throw these defective copies away, I decided to hang on to them for a while.

One day I ran into Lance, a former colleague of mine. We decided to go have coffee since Lance wanted to talk about how I had published the book. In our discussion I mentioned that I had some defective books I was trying to put to good use. Lance jokingly said something silly like "Send them to people whom you don't like." When someone says something silly or foolish, I have an urge to do better. So I responded by saying, "I can do better than that; I can cut these books in half and mail either a top half or bottom half to people."

That night when I went home and retired for the night, I couldn't sleep because I hadn't followed one of my important principles of creativity: Write down all ideas. I got out of bed and wrote, "Cut books in half and send to people" in my little black book. A week later I was trying to decide how to get companies more interested in my book and seminars. I didn't want to send any more free books since the response was not all that good. I happened to look in my black book and saw "Cut books in half and send to people."

This is exactly what I did. First, I went down to my printer and had him cut the books in half. Then, I drafted the following letter. Of course, my voice of judgment jumped in and tried to convince me this was a "dumb idea," which wouldn't work and wouldn't be good for my image. However, after some PMI analysis, I decided to be unreasonable and do it anyway. Sure, I knew some people would think I was crazy or unprofessional. But I also knew a lot of people would remember me. In addition, my curiosity was getting the best of me; I was wondering how people would respond to receiving either a top or bottom half of my book. I felt a little silly while stuffing half-books in envelopes. In the end, this silly promotion was well worth the effort.

Mr. Richard Strass
Capital Credit Corporation
Toronto, Ontario, M4W 1E6

Dear Mr. Strass:

You have just received half of my book, *The Art of Seeing Double or Better in Business.*

Why did I send you half a book? I had two problems: One, I had a few defective books, which I wanted to use for something other than fill in my garbage can. Two, I needed some way to get you interested in my book and seminars.

So I decided to be creative. By cutting the books in half, I solved both problems. First, I found a use for the defective books. Second, with all the material you receive, half a book has attracted your attention more so than other conventional marketing devices would have.

Incidentally, creativity is the foundation for *The Art of Seeing Double or Better in Business,* which was written to help people and organizations be more innovative. To increase productivity, many organizations are giving the book to their employees. Radio stations, credit unions, school boards, professional associations, and universities have purchased the book in bulk.

The book is available only directly from me through my seminars or with purchases of ten or more (twenty after July 1). A price list and order form are enclosed. Information about my seminars is also enclosed.

Sincerely,

Ernie J. Zelinski

Sending the half-books with the above letter resulted in several orders for ten books, which further led to sales of 200 books as well as several seminar presentations for one client. The extra revenues totaled between $10,000 and $20,000. I also received a lot of valuable publicity via newspaper articles, which led to other seminars and book sales. In fact, considering the profits this crazy idea generated, I found out I can cut perfectly good books in half and still have this type of promotion be very profitable.

There Is Reason to Be Unreasonable

Society and our educational institutions teach us to be reasonable and practical. Being reasonable and practical is a fine alternative if we are talking about not doing something stupid like jumping off a cliff. The problem is that society wants us to be "reasonable" in ways that hinder our creativity.

Albert Einstein stated, "Great spirits have always encountered violent opposition from mediocre minds." When we are considering something new and different, we don't have to look far to have someone tell us we are being unreasonable. We must be on guard and reject reason. Following the reason of others has wrecked many individuals' plans.

Creativity Principle:

Be Unreasonable

If we are to create anything that makes a difference in this world, we must also learn to challenge our own reasonableness. Remember that our own voices of judgment can be an enemy of our plans. Our own reasons for not doing something should constantly be challenged if we are to succeed in our creative endeavors.

I personally have found that "being unreasonable" is something that can be done on a daily basis. When I encounter either my own voice of judgment or someone else's, I try to go against the prevailing reason. By being unreasonable, I find some surprising and rewarding events occur.

One time I decided to be unreasonable and go talk to a professor who had given me a much lower grade than I thought I deserved on a midterm paper. What made my going to see him unreasonable was that at least four other students in his class felt the same way about their marks and had already gone to see him. He became very defensive and refused to give any of them any consideration for a higher mark. My unreasonableness paid off. I was able to get consideration from him despite four other students having tried before me. I just did things a little differently. I did not make him wrong by saying that he graded my paper unfairly. Instead, I said to him, "I messed up my last paper, which means I won't get a good final mark in this course. This will cost me an assistantship worth $3,000. What would you do if you were in my shoes?" He responded by reducing the weight of the midterm paper and putting more weight on the final. I wound up with honors and my $3,000.

> Nothing is ever accomplished by a reasonable man.
> — *American Proverb*

Be Reasonable and Have an Unreasonable Day

Society and our educational institutions programmed us to be reasonable. The problem is we become too reasonable. Our voices of judgment promptly label many ideas "unreasonable," when in fact, the ideas may have great merit. Being unreasonable, and doing what others wouldn't consider, can generate remarkable results as the following two examples indicate.

In 1989 Tennessee resident Jane Berzynsky read a tabloid's account of actor Bob Cummings's fourth divorce. She decided to be unreasonable and write to him, although she had never met him or talked to him on the phone. In her letter, she said that she was available if he wanted to consider a relationship with her. A photo was also included with the letter. Cummings, a Gemini, checked Berzynsky's Aquarius sign out with his astrologer. She checked out astrologically, so he flew her to Los Angeles. Jane Berzynsky ended up becoming Bob Cummings's fifth wife because she was willing to do something that was considered unreasonable by most people.

In April 1995, radio host Pierre Brassard of CKOI-FM in Montreal also did something totally unreasonable. He decided to call the Vatican in an attempt to talk to Pope John Paul. Even a high-ranking cardinal in Montreal said he wouldn't ever think of trying to call the pope. Brassard's staff ended up getting the pope on the line by using a little deceit (the staff chose to call it creativity). They claimed Brassard was Jean Chretien, the prime minister of Canada.

A telephone conversation in French between Brassard and the pope lasted about eighteen minutes; it was mostly small talk going nowhere. At one point Brassard asked the pope when he was going to get a propeller for his cap, but the pope didn't seem to understand the question. Reporters from media outlets all around North America were envious of what Brassard had done. Many other radio stations then tried to get an interview with the pope, but to no avail. Producers from TNN and the *Late Night with David Letterman* ended up calling CKOI-FM wanting to get a tape of the conversation between Brassard and the pope.

> Let's drink a toast to folly and to dreams because they are the only reasonable things.
> — *Paul-Loup Sulitzer*

We are all victims of our voices of judgment, the rational part of us that can jump in and destroy an idea before it has a chance to blossom. Many good ideas aren't given any chance. We tend to find something negative about these ideas and promptly discard them. The reverse is also true. We may promptly accept an idea without looking at all the negatives. Our voices of judgment work to classify things as black and white. We end up spending 95 percent of our time judging people and events whether they are bad or good, and right or wrong.

If you designate one day every week as your unreasonable day, and go through that day challenging your voice of judgment, you will notice life is different. I have selected Thursday as my unreasonable day. On Thursdays, I continually question my voice of judgment. With all the success I have had in arranging interviews that I initially thought I couldn't get, and getting to know people I didn't think I could meet, I have concluded it is very reasonable to be unreasonable. Here are some unreasonable things to do on your unreasonable day:

> No excellent soul is exempt from a mixture of madness.
> — *Aristotle*

- If you know someone who has the ideal job and would like to talk to them, telephone them on your unreasonable day.
- Surprise someone with a totally different deed or gift.
- Say something complimentary to the cashier at the grocery or department store.
- Learn to go against the trend in whatever you are doing or trying to accomplish.

What If We Ask Dumb Questions?

Seventeenth-century French writer Blaise Pascal felt that the only reason people ever do anything is to avoid thinking. This may be because people's minds aren't in condition to think. Pascal felt that by avoiding thinking people were avoiding the human condition characterized by inconsistency, boredom, and anxiety.

When you ask a dumb question, you get a smart answer.

— Aristotle

We regularly work on our houses. We regularly repair our cars. We keep up our bicycles. Some of us even regularly condition our bodies, but few of us regularly condition our minds. Regularly conditioning our minds can be as beneficial as regularly conditioning our bodies. Many people are in great physical condition, but their minds aren't in equally great condition. The ability to think critically and creatively is a rarely developed ability.

Jean-Paul Sartre said, "Existence is absurd." All existence may not be absurd, but a lot of human behavior is extremely absurd. One reason for this absurdity is people never stop to question their own behavior by asking dumb — or smart — questions. We don't stop to question why we are doing or thinking things that could be considered silly or suspect.

As children, we asked many dumb questions. We were curious and saw much wonder in this world. As adults, we can continue to challenge our minds with the new and mysterious by asking dumb questions, which often are more penetrating than smart questions.

I'm not an answering machine. I'm a questioning machine. If we have all the answers, how come we're in such a mess.

— Douglas Cardinal

If we continue to ask at least one dumb question a day, there can be much wonder in our lives until the day we die. We don't know everything there is to know (although a lot of us think we do). In fact, dumb minds have an answer for everything, while smart minds regularly ask dumb questions.

One of the best ways to practice being unreasonable is to ask random "what if" questions. These are questions that may sound absurd and unreasonable. Nonetheless, "what if's" can lead us to some interesting notions.

One day in the 1930s, Sylvan N. Goldman, a manager of a supermarket in Oklahoma City, was walking to work, when he saw two folding chairs facing each other on the lawn. He immediately thought, "What if I put folding chairs together, put a strip of wood on the seats, put more wood on the sides, and put wheels on the chairs? This giant basket with wheels may be an alternative to filled shopping baskets, which the customers often find too heavy and cumbersome to carry to the cashiers."

Because Goldman asked the important what-if question and followed through with the idea, on June 4, 1937, he introduced the world's first shopping cart on wheels for use in supermarkets.

Creative people asking what-if questions have led to many important inventions that we all take for granted today. The telephone, automobile windshield wipers, Velcro fasteners, french fries, and the ballpoint pen wouldn't have been discovered without their respective inventors asking what-if questions. Note that what-if questions can be used to solve all sorts of problems, including personal problems. Here are some examples of what-if questions:

- What if we marketed our product with something unrelated?
- What if we invited our top customers to our Christmas party?
- What if I took a year off work to travel to foreign countries?
- What if I leave home five minutes earlier to get to work?

Benefits of What-If Questions

- First, we get the opportunity to explore certain possibilities that we would not otherwise explore.
- Second, what-if questions may lead us to ideas altogether different from the one we started with.
- Last, what-if questions are a lot of fun.

A creative mind is an active mind, and an active mind asks many questions. Only through active questioning can we keep our minds developing and discovering new ways of thinking. Questioning our values, questioning our beliefs, and questioning why we are doing things the way we are doing them should be normal. Socrates, a great thinker in his time, encouraged his students to question everything, including what he was teaching them. You should use your mind in active ways to ensure you aren't letting it rust away. You must use it or lose it!

CHAPTER 13

Don't Put Off Your Procrastinating

Procrastinate and Be More Creative

One of the best ways for us to be more creative is to slow down and take our time in doing some tasks. We can actually be more productive by slowing down. Even procrastinating has its merits. By putting things off, we can be more efficient. This chapter is, in part, about the art of procrastination.

Attempt the following exercise to test your creativity.

Exercise 13-1. Twice as Fishy but Just as Square

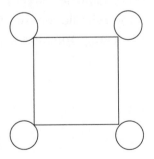

Who longest waits most
surely wins.

— *Helen Hunt Jackson*

Ms. Colleen Waller, a wealthy businesswoman, had a lovely square fishpond on her Toronto estate. On each corner of the fishpond was a round lily pond, as shown above. Colleen wanted to double the size of her fishpond to accommodate twice as many fish; however, she didn't want to disturb her four lily ponds. Colleen wanted to keep the fishpond square. The lily ponds were required to be outside the perimeter of the fishpond.

She spoke to her gardener about this. He said it was impossible, and all four lily ponds would have to be moved. How many lily ponds would you move?

Allow yourself thirty seconds to complete this problem.

What solution did you arrive at? Did you come to the conclusion that at least one lily pond didn't have to be moved? Optimally, no lily ponds have to be moved. There is a solution that makes this possible (see Appendix, page 182). Did you get this solution? If not, why not? You probably didn't get this better solution because I didn't allow you enough time. More time would have given you more opportunity to "see the light."

Taking too little time with a problem is something most of us do too often. In doing so, we wind up with solutions that are, at worst, totally unworkable and, at best, lacking in effectiveness. We must discipline ourselves to avoid rushing through situations when we can afford extra time for generating ideas. Sufficient time should be given for the generation of a large number of solutions. This necessitates delayed decision making.

Your Honor, the jury members request the rest of the summer to think about it.

Delaying action on problems can be very important for generating highly creative solutions. Too often, we rush solving a problem when we would be better off to wait. Many problems and situations aren't as urgent as we make them out to be. When they aren't, it's best for us to take the time to let our minds play with the problem. Then our minds can report back at a later day.

Exercise 13-2. Can You Remember Back When?

Assume that you have been given the task of planning a class reunion for all your classmates from grade one to grade four. How many names can you think of in the next five minutes?

How many did you get? Ten to twenty? How many classmates did you have in those four years? Some of them moved. Some new ones joined your class over that period. You probably have missed naming a number of them. If you are given the rest of the day to think of all of them, you will undoubtedly get more names. Names will even come to you when you are thinking about something else. At the end of the day you may have thought of 60 percent of the classmates that you had.

Then tomorrow you will think of more names if you are still focusing on this task. Of course, again, some names will come to you while thinking about other things. Eventually, after two or three days, you will have remembered most of your former classmates.

Giving time for incubation of ideas works in much the same way as trying to think of your classmates' names over a long time period. Your subconscious mind is given a chance to generate more ideas than if you consciously try to come up with all available solutions in a short period of time. Sudden ideas generated in a limited time span tend to be the product of structured and rational thinking processes. Incubation over a long period of time overcomes the constraints of short-term decision making.

Try the following exercise, allowing yourself two minutes.

> Ideas, like young wine, should be put in storage and taken up only after they have been given time to ferment and ripen.
>
> — *Richard Strauss*

Exercise 13-3. Breaking the Chain of Demand

A wealthy businessman and his chauffeur are robbed on their way to the city by a group of modern-day bandits. Their limousine and nearly all of their possessions are stolen. All the businessman has left of any value is a gold chain with twenty-three links. The businessman is too old to walk long distances. He finds the nearest hotel and sends his chauffeur for money and a new car. The chauffeur will take twenty-three days to fetch a car and some money and return. The hotel owner demands that the businessman give him one gold link each day as security for future payment. The businessman does not want to give the hotel owner more links than the number of nights he has stayed at the hotel. He wants to recover his chain with the fewest possible links that have been cut. What must the businessman do to give the hotel owner one link a day but cut as few links as possible?

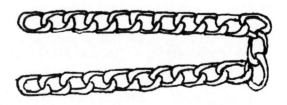

If you did what most people do with the above exercise, you determined that every second link had to be cut. This gives the minimum number cut as eleven. Actually there is a better solution with a lower number of required cuts. If you take your time and approach this problem from other perspectives, you may see the optimal solution. Try it. We'll come back to this later.

Creativity Principle:
Delay Your Decision

Incubation involves putting the problem on the back burner. This allows us to attend to other matters while the problem simmers away in our subconscious. We get away from direct involvement with the problem. In this way we suspend judgment and allow ourselves the luxury of having the problem travel through our various states of mind. In time, we will have had several solutions come and go at unexpected times. Because these solutions will just pop out of nowhere, it is important that we write them down. Otherwise, we stand the chance of forgetting some excellent solutions.

Allowing more time results in our experiencing greater perception. Associations with other stimulants generate new perspectives that we do not experience when we rush through the problem. We avoid the rigidity that we have in the initial stages. This results in new and more open observations, which lead to interesting and sometimes stunning ideas.

In solving exercise 13-3, you can just accept that eleven links have to be cut. However, if you decide to take more time, you likely will get a better solution. If you put this problem on the back burner of your mind, tomorrow or another day the solution can hit you out of nowhere. Suppose you are in a store paying for a two-dollar item with a five-dollar bill. The clerk gives you three dollars (in one-dollar bills) back. An association of this transaction can be made to the problem of the businessman with the gold chain. Where may this lead?

At this point it may occur to you that this type of transaction can be made by the businessman and the hotel owner, only it will be with gold links and not dollars. (Hint: On a particular day, does the businessman have to deal with a denomination of only one gold link? Can't he give a higher denomination, say three links together, and get change, two single links, back? Where will this thinking lead? Now play around with the problem for a better solution. The optimal solution to the problem is that only two links have to be cut. See if you can figure out which two links these are.)

> Patience is the art of concealing your impatience.
>
> — *Unknown Wise Person*

For most problems, various associations with unrelated items can be made during the incubation stage. This may lead to several good answers. A new problem may also arise. The problem may be that of choosing the best answer from the many outstanding ones you have generated. This is a good problem to have.

Generating More Stunning Solutions by Slowing Down

Disciplining yourself to avoid rushing through a problem is the first step in finding stunning or blockbuster solutions. This requires the presence of mind to convince yourself that the world is not going to come to an end if you do not make a decision today. Some problem solving is urgent; some is not. Once you have decided that you have the luxury of additional time, you are well on your way to finding a better answer. We saw how taking time with exercise 13-3 can lead to a much better solution (see Appendix, page 182, for the exact solution).

A story must simmer in its own juice for months or even years before it's ready to serve.

— *Edna Ferber*

Looking for better solutions can be done consciously, by stating the problem to yourself for several days. Reminding yourself of the problem can be done in many ways. Here are some of the ways to consciously attend to the problem in preparation for letting your subconscious mind do the work to find a blockbuster solution.

- Write your problem on several strips of paper. Leave these strips in various locations so that you come across them from time to time. Leave one in your briefcase, one in the medicine cabinet, one on the car dash, one on your office desk, and so on. In this way you will be reminded about your problem unexpectedly.

- Remind yourself of the problem while performing physical activities. Do this while walking, exercising, cleaning the house, or shoveling the walk. Whisper your problem while shaving or putting your makeup on.

- State your problem while meditating in private, daydreaming in your office, or resting on the sofa.

- State your problem to yourself the first thing in the morning, after you get up. State it a second time and then leave it alone for a while.

It is important to note that you are not being asked to worry about your problem day and night. You are to consciously think about the problem at the various times with full confidence that an answer will appear in due time.

After several days of consciously thinking about your problem, the stunning answer may have appeared. If it has, the mission is complete. If it hasn't, then stop thinking about the problem consciously. Allow the problem to simmer in your subconscious for some time after. Seemingly, out of nowhere, answers will appear. Eventually, one will surface with a stunning effect. Eureka! Intuitively, you will know that this is the great one.

Be Persistent and Wind Up a Genius

Genius Is Nothing More than Persistence Disguised

Throughout this book I have emphasized several principles of creativity and other tidbits of information for achieving satisfaction in life. The only principle of creativity not yet discussed in detail is just as important as any of the principles and tidbits already discussed. The following two examples emphasize the last principle of creativity, which is "Be persistent."

Do you recognize any of these names? Captain Betts, Willie Delight, Jed Jackson, Buddy Links, Jimmy Malone, and Willy Williams. These were all stage names George Burns used early in his career as a vaudeville comedian. Burns admitted his acts were so bad that he frequently had to change his name to get booked again. However, his persistence paid off. Burns eventually developed an act people loved, and he became a star.

If at first you don't succeed, you're about average.

— Unknown Wise Person

Thomas Edison is reported to have made several hundred experiments before he was successful in developing the lightbulb. After about 500 attempts, Edison's assistant asked him, "Why do you persist in this folly? You have tried 500 times, and you have failed 500 times." Edison was quick to respond. "Oh, but I have not failed even once. Now I know

500 ways how not to make a lightbulb." Of course, Edison's persistence eventually paid off with a workable lightbulb.

The power of persistence is remarkable. I can vouch for the power of persistence or perseverance. Today my books sell in the tens of thousands in U.S. and Canadian bookstores. I accept a few speaking engagements paying as much as $2,000 plus expenses for a half hour. Sometimes I turn down certain lucrative speaking engagements because my leisure time is more important. Yet as recently as five years ago I would have gladly shared with you much of the information contained in my speeches and books for free. In fact, I would have treated you to an expensive dinner just so I could have someone to listen to me. (I was desperate to have someone on whom I could test my material.)

Creativity Principle:

Be Persistent

I recall, several years ago, sitting with a group of acquaintances in a restaurant, discussing what it takes to be successful in life. When I stated my philosophy about creativity and what constitutes security in life, everyone else at the table told me I was either weird or crazy. When I was in the MBA program at the University of Alberta, I challenged the academics to change the outdated program and put creativity courses in it. Most MBA students and professors thought I was, if not a total basket case, then certainly on a different page than they were.

Despite the criticism I have taken over the last few years, I was able to follow my own philosophy and make it work to my advantage. One of the biggest reasons for my zest for living today is I enjoy what I do for a living. Since I don't have to work more than four or five hours a day, I also have a great balance between work and play. In fact, most of my work is play, since I enjoy it so much. I wouldn't take a salary of $1 million a year to work for anyone else, no matter what the job or title, simply because I enjoy my freedom.

How did I get to where I am? I got here by being persistent. While the people with whom I graduated from the MBA program were making $75,000 a year, I was making $15,000 a year. I persevered even when I was living at the poverty level and didn't know where my next month's rent was coming from. I always felt if I stuck to what I enjoyed I could eventually make a living at it.

Now some people who, a few years ago, thought my mental elevator didn't go to the top floor are willing to pay me for advice. Certain individuals from my graduating class think I am a marketing genius because I was able to make a self-published book a best-seller. I am no more a genius in marketing (or anything else for that matter) than other individuals with some knowledge of marketing and some common sense. What has helped me attain some of my important goals is my willingness to be persistent and my willingness to follow the other sixteen principles of creativity.

> Persistence is what makes the impossible possible, the possible likely, and the likely definite.
>
> — *Robert Half*

You can do the same with your life. Persist in your plans and endeavors, and you may wind up a genius (or a star) in the eyes of others less persistent than you. At that point you will know that genius is nothing more than persistence or perseverance disguised.

Don't Be a Victim of Incorrect Thinking

A great mystery to me is why so many people choose to blame the world instead of taking responsibility for their lives. A *Globe and Mail* editorial recently stated that the 1990s is the decade of the victim. Since it is even trendy in some social circles to be a victim, I must take the time to warn you of the potential consequences, in case you ever come close to falling into the mental trap of unnecessarily thinking you are a victim.

Many people look at themselves as victims when, in fact, they aren't. These individuals look at life as a rip-off due to their position if life. They blame society, their parents, their country's economic state, or the world in general for their unhappiness and loneliness.

> The losing horse blames the saddle.
>
> — *Samuel Lover*

The thing that impresses me about people with the victim mentality is how much energy they will put into shunning responsibility and complicating their lives.

Victims tend to be people driven by negative motivation. Affected by their own insecurities and past failures, people with negative motivation in life just go through the motions. They complain all the time, start things and don't finish them, make the same mistakes again and again, and nothing around them seems to work. The saddest thing is they aren't aware of how negative they are.

About ten years ago, I was surprised when a fifty-five-year-old man told me that he still blamed his parents for a lot of the troubles in his life, including his failed relationships. I thought this was a little strange for a man of fifty-five whose parents had been dead for years and who had children of his own. Much to my further surprise, since that time ten years ago, parent bashing has become acceptable. In the 1990s, it has even become a trendy pastime for many adults, as manifested by the coverage on TV talk shows and psychology magazines. The parent bashers refer to themselves as "adult children" (a rather curious term indeed).

These adult children have been known to pass blame for their own current problems in adulthood, such as alcoholism, drug addiction, divorce, and incompatible relationships, onto their parents. What is wrong with this? Adult children are unwilling to take responsibility for their own actions. They suffer from a victim mentality and attempt to shun responsibility for anything and everything distasteful in their lives.

> Take your life in your own hands, and what happens? A terrible thing: no one to blame.
>
> — *Erica Jong*

To show how absurd it is for these adult children to blame their parents for their problems, let me go back to a seminar in which I participated a few years ago. During the seminar proceedings, one of the 257 participants was confronted by the seminar leader when the participant mentioned that many of his personal problems were due to his less-than-perfect parents. To emphasize to this misguided participant how wrong he was to think that he was disadvantaged because of his parents, the seminar leader asked the rest of the 256 participants to raise our hands if we thought that we had excellent or close-to-perfect parents. Much to the surprise of this participant, not one hand went up. As the seminar leader pointed out, the 257 participants represented a wide range of backgrounds, and not one of them had even remotely perfect parents.

Michele Wiener-Davis, a well-known professional therapist, has shown great integrity in writing her excellent book *Fire Your Shrink,* in which she talks about the dangers of the victim mentality and why therapy usually doesn't work for most people who see "shrinks." Many people with the victim mentality spend countless hours fixating on their problems in the company of highly paid therapists. As Michele Wiener-Davis has discovered, people with the victim mentality spend months, or even years, passing blame, and never get around to taking responsibility for actually solving their problems. Of course, therapists benefit from clients not having solved their problems, because the clients keep coming back with money in their hands.

> Life is short, but it's long enough to ruin any man who wants to be ruined.
>
> — *Josh Billings*

There are many thinking patterns that signal low self-esteem. If you have any of the following beliefs or thoughts, you are subjecting yourself to negative motivators that won't contribute anything to your success.

- I have problems in life that are unique. Nobody else could possibly have these whoppers.
- You can't tell me anything that I don't already know.
  - When someone dislikes me, I feel bad about myself.
  - I should not be subject to the discomfort of failure.
  - The world ought to be fair, especially to me.
  - People are so different from the way they should be.
  - Changing myself is impossible because I was born this way.
- My less-than-perfect parents are to blame for the way I am.
- Governments don't do enough for common people like myself.
- Governments should do more to protect our jobs in the health, teaching, _____, etc. fields.
- I am at a disadvantage because I am a woman, a member of a minority, a white male, _____, etc.
- I am disadvantaged because I do not have enough money, am not beautiful, and don't know the right people.
- Why isn't everyone as nice to me as I am to everyone else?
- I don't have enough education to accomplish anything.
- I have trouble asserting myself.

> When you see a snake, never mind where he came from.
> — W. G. Benham

If you regularly have any of the above thoughts, you are setting yourself up for much grief and pain. You are consciously or subconsciously generating excuses for not taking the steps you must take to make your life work. You are also a victim of incorrect thinking. Whose? Your own! Who else's?

In her book, Wiener-Davis writes about people who used to suffer from the victim mentality and now have become winners by turning their lives around. She states, "People who live their dreams are those who stop considering all the angles, weighing the pros and cons, and just do it.... They've come to realize it's time to stop talking to their friends, families, or therapists, ... and begin living. Without action there is no change."

> If your daily life seems poor, do not blame it; blame yourself. Tell yourself that you are not poet enough to call forth its riches.
> — Rainer Maria Rilke

Belief Is a Disease

Just because the majority in society holds a belief, the belief isn't necessarily true. What society considers reasonable may actually be very unreasonable. Many people have held false beliefs before. Remember that nearly all of humankind at one time thought the world was flat. This point made by Bertrand Russell offers much food for thought.

BIZARRO

> The fact that an opinion has been widely held is no evidence whatever that it is not entirely absurd; indeed in view of the silliness of the majority of mankind, a widespread belief is more likely to be foolish than sensible.

Our failure to be questioning machines can result in our adopting many false beliefs about life. It is easy to fall for false beliefs common in society. Here are two examples: Do you believe reading in the dark or in poor light will hurt your eyes? Guess what? There is no evidence to support this. The American Academy of Ophthalmology states: "Reading in dim light can no more harm your eyes than taking a photograph in dim light can harm the camera."

Do you believe that it is dangerous to go swimming right after you eat a large meal? Here again, there is no evidence to support this. Although the Red Cross published a brochure fifty years ago warning of the danger associated with eating before swimming, today's Red Cross brochure says it isn't dangerous to swim after eating.

Worse than having a false belief here and there is living a life based on what reality ought to be, instead of what it is. Writer Robert DeRopp stated that human beings inhabit a world of delusions, which obscures reality to such an extent that they are living in a world of waking dreams. The fear of the truth can be unshakable to certain individuals. People will go to great lengths to avoid the truth and replace it with some wild fantasy that will make any sane person's brain spin.

> I never cease being dumbfounded by the unbelievable things people believe.
> — *Leo Rosten*

Most of us tend to structure our thinking patterns in ways that prevent us from seeing all the possibilities for solutions to life's problems, with a great impact on our creative abilities. Being a creative individual means living with passion and spontaneity. Trusting your intuition is important; so is knowing when to suspend your preconceptions and inhibitions.

Flexible thinking will help you get through life with greater ease; don't get stuck in your beliefs. A belief that life will be better with a big lottery win is a disease. If you don't stop and question all your beliefs about life now and then, your structured thinking can be detrimental to your mental health. Structured thinking will limit your ability to see things in a different light. Remember, your mind is like a parachute — you are far better off when it is open.

Everything that deceives may be said to enchant.

— Plato

Liberation Is a State of Mind

Winning at life takes action and achievement. The ability to be successful isn't something anyone is born with. People can lead fulfilling lives, if they take responsibility for themselves and refrain from thinking of themselves as victims. Instead of justifying why they are victims, and ending up in a prison, creative individuals look for opportunities, take advantage of them, and end up in a paradise.

Liberty means responsibility. That's why most men dread it.

— George Bernard Shaw

Negative people have a desire for comfort and a desire to avoid failure, which usually results in low intention, or complete inaction. Although fear can be a positive motivator, more often than not it negatively motivates us to react in ways that contribute little or nothing to our satisfaction. Fear, for the most part, induces us to react negatively, rather than positively.

Other unhealthy modes of thinking, such as the one-big-deal syndrome, act as negative motivation. The one-big-deal syndrome is one of those adolescent-rescue fantasies we all had in our younger years. Unfortunately, I know many people who have carried these adolescent-rescue fantasies well into their fifties and sixties. Adolescent fantasies are favorites of adults with low self-esteem.

Success doesn't come to you. . . . You go to it.

— Marve Collins

These are some variations of the one-big-deal syndrome: If I could only win a five-million-dollar lottery, then I would be happy; if I could only get a new relationship with someone exciting, then I wouldn't be so bored; and if I could get an exciting, high-paying job, then I could start living. People afflicted with the one-big-deal syndrome are looking for an easy way to happiness, when none exists. Waiting for the one big deal avoids the effort required to make life work.

Excuses are valid if you are severely handicapped or if you live in a Third World country with virtually no opportunity. The United States and Canada still offer incredible opportunity for capable individuals. In 1997, for the fourth straight year, Canada was chosen by the United Nations as the best place to live in the world in terms of the human development index; the United States was chosen fourth overall in 1997. The ranking was based on average income, life expectancy, and educational attainment.

> If you don't want to do something, one excuse is as good as another.
> — *Yiddish Saying*

Despite Canada's ranking as the best place in the world to live, I find many people don't see the opportunity that exists in the country. Many Canadians spend most of their time complaining about how bad things are and how rough life is. And most of these people I am talking about aren't severely disadvantaged. I am talking about healthy, able, well-educated, and previously or presently highly paid individuals who are spoiled and suffer from the-world-owes-me-a-living syndrome.

I point to what Douglas Cardinal, probably Canada's most renowned architect, recently said. Cardinal, of native Indian heritage, believes we have something to learn from his philosophy:

> We don't have an economic problem but an attitude problem. We're splashing around feeling sorry for ourselves because our economy is down. What a bunch of nonsense. That's an attitude. We've got an attitude problem. The doom and gloom doesn't affect me because I refuse to participate. . . . We can create anything we wish. It's our own attitude that puts us in the situation we're in. Those laid off from jobs can see their predicaments as setbacks or challenges.

> "They're Only Puttin' in a Nickel, but They Want a Dollar Song"
> — *Song Title*

I must warn you of the most dangerous effect of the victim mentality. You will never be liberated if this is your game in life. How can you? You will always set it up so that you are a victim, to satisfy your perverted belief system.

Liberation is a state of mind. If you are a truly liberated person, you know there is discrimination of all sorts out there, as well as many other roadblocks; however, you will decide to go for it anyway. Liberation takes effort and persistence — not someone else's but your own.

To Know and Not to Do Is Not Yet to Know

Many unmotivated people suffer from a delusion about the existence of that promised land about halfway between Nirvana and Shangri-la; they believe that they can reach it without any effort. All it will take is one big deal in life in the form of a big lottery win, landing the ideal job, or finding the right marriage partner. The one-big-deal-in-life syndrome stems from false beliefs about the way the world ought to be, instead of seeing it as it is. People suffering from the one-big-deal-in-life syndrome live a life based on part truth and part fiction. The fiction entails what ought to be. Living a life based mainly on what the world ought to be — instead of the way it is — can be self-destructive; in fact, the consequences are usually quite severe.

> Don't go around saying the world owes you a living; the world owes you nothing. It was here first.
>
> — Mark Twain

I trust that you won't fall into the same trap as so many unmotivated people fall into. Throughout their lives they suffer from the world-owes-me-a-living and windfall-from-nowhere syndromes. Assuming they don't have to take responsibility for their well-being, these people continually look for the easy way out. That's why so many North Americans are addicted to gambling, drugs, and alcohol. Most of us had the windfall-from-nowhere urge at one time or another. A long time ago, I used to imagine receiving windfalls from nowhere; now, this doesn't happen to me much, if at all. I realize that there is no such thing as a windfall from nowhere. Besides, I found out that I don't need a windfall from nowhere to experience satisfaction and happiness in my life. I can accomplish this by using my creativity and following the Easy Rule of Life.

> For one person who dreams of making 50,000 pounds, a hundred people dream of being left 50,000 pounds.
>
> — A. A. Milne

Having learned the principles of creativity won't guarantee that you will gain more success and satisfaction from life — just as owning a horse won't guarantee you will ride the horse and appreciate it — you have to motivate yourself in some way to do what is necessary to attain satisfaction at anything worth doing. You must also forget the excuses.

Exercise 14-1. A Common Nonexcuse

What did these people all have in common?

- Thomas Edison (inventor)
- Sophia Loren (actor)
- Al Pacino (actor)
- Bobby Fisher (former world chess champion)
- Peter Jennings (TV newscaster on ABC)
- Soichiro Honda (founder of Honda Motor Corp.)
- Buckminster Fuller (inventor of geodesic dome)

Many people use the excuse of their limited education for not pursuing more creative and satisfying careers. Well, guess what? All of the above people were either elementary or high school dropouts. Thomas Edison had only three weeks of formal education. Another handicap was deafness from which he suffered for most of his life. Did this stop him? No! His inventions dramatically changed our lives.

Success is that old ABC — ability, breaks, and courage.

— Charles Luckman

So let's forget the excuses. Just because something is difficult is no reason for not doing it. It is one thing to acknowledge problems in life and decide what must be done to change — most people can reach this point — where most people fail is in doing something about it. Inaction renders the knowledge of the problem and what to do about it worthless. There is an old saying, "Talk is cheap because supply exceeds demand." Many people talk about the wonderful things they are going to do in life but never get around to doing very many of them. Talking about the walk is one thing; walking the talk is another issue in itself.

Never, never, never, never, give up!

— Winston Churchill

The difference between high achievers and low achievers is that high achievers think actively and not passively. Studies of high achievers indicate they can take a lot of time to just think about things. Their accomplishment is not based only on being physically active, but also on their ability to meditate, ponder, and daydream.

Achievers think about being doers and attaining a sense of accomplishment. Eventually, they do what they have been planning to do; this makes the difference in their lives. They know making a difference, whether in leisure pursuits or in business affairs, means having to light the fire rather than just waiting around to be warmed by someone else's fire.

Walking the talk is about commitment. Many people use the word *commitment* but they don't really know what it means. Using the word, because it sounds nice, doesn't mean you're committed. The majority say they are committed to being happy and successful in life. Their actions prove the opposite. When they learn their goal requires time, energy, and sacrifice, they give up the goal.

Don't wait for your ship to come in. Swim out to it.

— Unknown Wise Person

Here is a simple test to determine how committed you are to your goals and making your life work: Do you do the things you say you are going to do? This applies to seemingly insignificant items like calling a person when you say you will. If you are not doing the small things that you say you will do, I have a hard time believing you will be committed to larger goals. If commitment is lacking in your life, you won't attain very much satisfaction in the long run.

Your actions are the only things that will attest to your commitment. A seriousness about commitment will mean you have the intense desire to achieve your goals, no matter what barrier or wall appears in your way. "As you sow, so shall you reap." In other words, whatever you put in the universe will be reflected back to you. It takes action — plenty of it — to get fulfillment and satisfaction in your life. Don't be like most people, who don't follow through with action. Your positive attitude and enthusiasm for living are the ingredients for being committed to action and a life that works. When it comes to commitment, always remember these words of wisdom from the Buddhists: "To know and not to do is not yet to know."

The great end of life is not knowledge but action.

— *Thomas Henry Huxley*

CHAPTER 15

Be a Creative Loafer Now and Zen

Is Time on Your Side?

In the book *The Little Prince* by Antoine de Saint-Exupéry, the little prince arrives from a foreign planet to visit the planet earth. One of the strange people the little prince encounters is a merchant who tries to sell him pills that allow people to quench their thirst and feel no need to drink anything for a week. The little prince asks the merchant why he is selling these pills. The merchant replies, "Because they save a tremendous amount of time. Computations have been made by experts. With these pills, you save fifty-three minutes in every week."

The little prince then asks, "And what do I do with those fifty-three minutes?" and the merchant replies, "Anything you like. . . ." The little prince in bewilderment says to himself, "As for me, if I had fifty-three minutes to spend as I liked, I should walk at my leisure toward a spring of fresh water."

This story has a lot to say about how we use our time and approach life. In North America, there never seems to be enough time. In this do-it-all society, people drive fast, walk fast, dine fast, and talk fast. Time is so precious that people don't even have a moment to think about time. Even leisure time is experienced in a

> Yesterday is a cancelled check; tomorrow is a promissory note; today is the only cash you have — so spend it wisely.
>
> — *Kay Lyons*

hurried state. No one can ride a horse, smoke a cigarette, read a book, and get laid all at the same time. Yet, it seems many individuals are trying to do just that. People have become so involved in controlling time that they can't find the time to enjoy the present moment. Because they don't have a moment to spare, they are less spontaneous and unable to enjoy the here and now.

Busy-ness doesn't mean you are in control. Being in the now means opening yourself to the moment in which there are no other moments. Thinking how much happier you would be if only you were richer or more beautiful isn't the way to enjoy life in the here and now. Waiting for something to happen so you can enjoy life means you aren't fully conscious of the world around you. Waiting for that one big deal in life to appear, so you can enjoy life, will result in your postponing the joys of living. If you can immerse yourself in the things you enjoy now, you will be happier now. You will start living in the moment, instead of just existing in a semiconscious state.

Get involved in the process, instead of the end result, and you will know that you are fully experiencing the moment. Learn to let go of the clock. Quiet and uninterrupted time is necessary to reduce the pressure and stress of modern-day life. When you are relaxed, you will be more positive in your outlook on life. Being unhurried means being different from the crowd. You will be more creative because you are able to enjoy the magic of the now.

Concentrating on Concentration

Being in the now is emphasized in Zen, an Eastern discipline, which has personal enlightenment as its goal. The following Zen story illustrates the importance of mastering the moment:

A student of Zen asked his teacher, "Master, what is Zen?" The master replied, "Zen is sweeping the floors when you sweep the floors, eating when you eat, and sleeping when you sleep." The student responded by

CALVIN AND HOBBES

saying, "Master, that is so simple." "Of course," said the master. "But so few people ever do it."

Most people are seldom in the present moment. They miss out on many opportunities in life. Having presence of mind, or paying attention to the moment, is something upon which most of us can improve, and from which we all can benefit. The ability to be in the now and concentrate on the task at hand is a very important aspect of the creative process for both work and play.

Creativity Principle:

Be in the now

Essential to your mastering the moment is learning to do one thing at a time, instead of two or three. Doing something physically and thinking about something else at the same time are contradictory. You aren't free to take part in your chosen activity if you are thinking about something else. One of the problems we have with leisure is choosing something and sticking with it until it is time to quit. Any act or task should be worthy of our total attention, if it is worth doing at all.

Test your ability to experience and live in the now by doing the following exercise:

Exercise 15-1. Contemplating a Paper Clip

Choose a simple object like a piece of chalk or a paper clip. Concentrate on the object for five minutes. Your task is not to let any other thoughts interfere with your thoughts about the object. In thinking about the object, think about the form as well as the concept behind the form. Where did the object come from? Who invented it? Why is it shaped the way it is?

Here is another good test for how well you can enjoy the moment: When taking a shower, try to eliminate all your thoughts about everything in your life. When you can get to a point where all you are experiencing is the pleasant and relaxing sound of the water running, you are truly experiencing a shower. When you try this, you will notice how easy it is to think about other things, many of which rob you of energy and the moment.

> The shortest way to do many things is to do only one thing at once.
> — *Samuel Smiles*

If you didn't do what was suggested in exercise 15-1 and instead kept on reading, you have shown how you are driven by your old self, so stop now. Go back and do the exercise! If you aren't able to do it, forget about being able to truly master the moment and just be. You are driven by external forces, which will continue to dominate the way you react.

If you did get around to doing exercise 15-1, how did you do? If you are like most people, you had trouble with wandering thoughts. You became critical, judgmental, or helpless in doing this ridiculous exercise. Having difficulty with this exercise indicates how your thinking is very much out of control. You don't have to despair. Practice can help you overcome this. You can develop the ability to be in the here and now, if you want to.

The following two exercises will help you develop your ability to be in the here and now. Individuals who have used these exercises report improvement in their ability to enjoy the moment.

Exercise 15-2. Concentrating on Concentration

Take a simple object and study it intently for five minutes every day. Concentrate on its form, as well as the form behind it. After two or three days, when you have totally explored the first object, use another simple object. Change objects as necessary. This exercise should be done for at least thirty days straight. The gestation period is this long, because this is how long it takes for our minds to change and develop better concentration. Every time you miss a day, you should go back to square one and try for thirty days straight. The benefits of this exercise cannot be explained in normal engineering or business school logic. Nevertheless, the benefits are real. Your subconscious faculties will open up to enable you to concentrate in ways you haven't concentrated before.

> Half of our life is spent trying to find something to do with the time we have rushed through life trying to save.
>
> — Will Rogers

Exercise 15-3. Clocking Your Concentration

Set the alarm of your clock or watch to go off at various times during the day to remind you to be in the here and now, so you can enjoy the moment. Use this as a reminder to have the presence of mind to get totally immersed in what you are doing. This can be a reminder to truly enjoy your work by doing one thing at a time. It may be a reminder to appreciate the taste of food by eating slowly. You may be reminded to fully experience a beautiful sunset, or to be totally present with the people around you. No matter what it is, try and do what you are doing completely, instead of doing it in a mediocre way while your mind is thousands of miles away.

Worrying about Matters That Don't Matter at All

A good way to miss the moment is to spend your time worrying about yesterday and tomorrow. There are many things to worry about. People have nervous breakdowns due to seemingly insignificant things, such as the television breaking down before the start of Oprah or having lost a few bucks in an investment scam. Some people even worry if they have nothing to worry about.

Think of many things to do — do one.

— Portuguese Proverb

The key is to put problems and worrying into proper perspective. Always thinking about the future and postponing things instead of doing them today means you are missing out on living today. If you think you will be happy in the future, when you get to do something drastically different, you're fooling yourself. Now is the time to be happy. Worrying about retirement and putting things off until then are risky, since you don't know if you will reach retirement age. Save your energy for the truly serious problems you have to solve. Fill your life with hope, dreams, and creative leisure instead of worry.

The ability to experience the here and now is a characteristic of creatively alive individuals. Creatively alive people are those who can get totally immersed in a project. Their concentration level is so high that they lose all sense of time. Their project totally envelopes them — having distracting thoughts isn't a problem. Their secret? They enjoy the moment for what it is, and don't worry about what is coming up next.

Nothing matters very much, and very few things matter at all.

— Arthur Balfour, Earl of Balfour

Worrying about the trivial or important is one of the activities that robs people of the now. About 15 percent of the U.S. public spends at least 50 percent of each day worrying, says a study from Pennsylvania State University. Worry is so rampant in North America that certain researchers claim approximately one out of three people in North American society has serious mental problems as a result of worrying.

Fear, anxiety, and guilt are emotions related to worrying. At any given time, at work or elsewhere, people's minds are far, far away — mostly thinking about worries and regrets. Most people are worrying about what happened yesterday or what will happen tomorrow.

Are you spending too much time worrying and missing out on today? Can you concentrate and be in the here and now? Spending too much time worrying about losing, failing, or making mistakes will make you tense and anxious. Too much worrying predisposes you to stress, headaches, panic attacks, ulcers, and other related ailments. Most worry is self-inflicted and somewhat useless.

Studies show that 40 percent of our worries are about events that will never happen, 30 percent of our worries are about events that already happened, 22 percent of our worries are about trivial events, 4 percent of our worries are about real events we cannot change, and only 4 percent of our worries are about real events on which we can act. This means that 96 percent of the things we worry about are things we can't control. Ninety-six percent of our worrying is wasted. In fact, it is even worse than that. Worrying about things we can control is wasted as well, since we can control these things. In other words, worrying about things we can't control is wasted because we can't control them, and worrying about things we can control is wasted because we can control these things. The result is 100 percent of our worrying is wasted. (Now you can worry about all the time you have been wasting while worrying.)

> Never cry over spilt milk. It could've been whiskey.
>
> — *Unknown Wise Person*

Spending time worrying about the past or future is a waste of energy. Creative people realize Murphy's Law has some bearing on the way things will be; that is, "If anything can go wrong, it will."

Hurdles are a certainty in life. Even the highly creative can't eliminate all the hurdles. They realize many new hurdles will appear regularly, but they also realize there is a way to overcome virtually all hurdles.

Most, if not all, worrying about problems robs you of energy that can be channeled to solve these problems. Here is a good attitude for you to adopt: Ultimately nothing matters and so what if it did? If you can live this motto, most worries will be eliminated.

Creatively alive people yield and go with the flow. In going with the flow, creatively alive people are acknowledging the importance of mastering the moment.

Being Bored Is an Insult to Oneself

Many uncreative individuals profess that handling boredom is their greatest source of anxiety. Free time is something they fear. They don't use their time effectively, and happiness escapes them. Instead of being participants in life, they specialize in being spectators and critics of other people's activities. Life becomes one continuous period of boredom and dejection. Boredom deprives people of the meaning of life and undermines their zest for living. Although it would seem to specifically affect those who are single or jobless, working and married people can be just as susceptible.

Being a spectator isn't the way to get the most out of life. You can't sit around and expect exciting things to happen to you. Only you can take responsibility for situating yourself in places where something is likely to happen. By planning and using your time wisely, you will be able to experience old and new activities that enhance the quality of your life.

Keeping busy doing the things you love will help you handle boredom. Taking on new and difficult tasks helps conquer boredom. You must be accountable for your boredom. Following is the complete content from a letter that I received from a professor in the faculty of the education department at a university in Western Canada who read *The Joy of Not Working:*

> Is not life a hundred times too short for us to bore ourselves?
> — *Friedrich Nietzsche*

Dear Mr. Zelinski:

I very much enjoyed your book, *The Joy of Not Working*. I decided that I am boring myself; I plan to do something about it.

Thank you.

John

From several hundred letters that I received about *The Joy of Not Working*, this letter is one of the most powerful, despite being the shortest. The chapter on boredom titled "Somebody Is Boring Me, I Think It Is Me" must have made an impact on John. He realized that there is only one person in his life who can do something about his boredom — John!

> I am never bored anywhere: being bored is an insult to oneself.
> — *Jules Renard*

Psychologists have determined that people who are chronically bored are conformists, worriers, lacking in self-confidence, uncreative, highly sensitive to criticism, and anxious for security and material things. Boredom is most likely to hit people who choose the safer, no-risk path in life. Because they take no risks, they seldom reap the payoffs of accomplishment, contentment, and satisfaction. People who choose the path of variety and stimulation are rarely stricken with the ailment of boredom. Creative individuals, who look for many things to do and many ways of doing them, find that life is tremendously exciting and worthwhile.

In modern times, boredom is thought to be externally imposed. However, the failure of our imaginations leads us into boredom. Things become boring because we expect them to be stimulating. People who require novelty in all their external activities are undoubtedly addicted to novelty. Due to their lack of imaginative thinking, many of these people try to evade the dullness of their daily lives by gambling, drinking, and taking drugs. People addicted to novelty are known to change jobs, marriage partners, and surroundings with reckless abandon. Because they don't use their imaginations, they continually wind up bored and dissatisfied.

Perfectionists, who set unrealistically high standards for life, are prime candidates for boredom, and even depression. They set these extremely high standards for their friends and themselves. Everything in life is supposed to be exciting and interesting. Perfectionists tend to set these standards for prospective marriage partners. If these prospective partners don't turn out to be charming, exceptionally attractive, and interesting, perfectionists get bored with these men or women; they eventually reject them because they are too boring, failing to recognize that the fault is with themselves.

> Life is too short to stuff a mushroom.
>
> — Storm Jameson

We must confront our boredom whenever it strikes. Only by using our imaginations can we overcome boredom. Your willingness to take responsibility for your boredom is the creative force that will eliminate boredom. Once you have accepted that your attitude determines the quality of your life, you are well on your way to eliminating boredom and dejection.

Lack of Spontaneity Is a Trait of the Dead

One way to learn to live the moment and overcome boredom is to be spontaneous now and then. Unlike the majority of adults, creatively alive adults can be spontaneous. Spontaneity is, for all intents and purposes, synonymous with creative living. Creatively alive people aren't inhibited; they can express their true feelings. They are able, like children, to play and act foolish. They also are able, on the spur of the moment, to decide to do something not in their plans for that day.

> Learn to enjoy the little things in life because the big ones don't come around very often.
>
> — Andy Rooney

How spontaneous are you? Do you always stick to your plans for the day? Do you always follow a set routine? How often do you ignore your plans and do something different?

I have found when I do something spontaneous, unexpected and interesting things happen to me. Many times I wind up with rewarding experiences that I would have never achieved by sticking to my plans.

Abraham Maslow, the famous humanist psychologist, believed spontaneity is a trait that is too often lost as people grow older. Maslow said, "Almost any child can compose a song or poem or a dance or a painting or a play or a game on the spur of the moment, without planning or previous intent." The majority of adults lose this ability, according to Maslow. Nevertheless, Maslow found a small fraction of adults did not lose this trait, and if they did, they regained it later in life. These are the self-actualized people, who have achieved a state of outstanding mental health. Maslow called this a state of being fully human. He found self-actualized people to be spontaneous and highly creative while moving toward maturity.

Watch children to refresh your notion of spontaneity. If you can be a child again, you can be spontaneous. Being spontaneous means challenging your plans; it means being able to try something new on the spur of the moment because it may be something you will enjoy. Although most accountants and engineers would probably try to plan to be more spontaneous, no one can plan spontaneity. "Planned spontaneity" is an oxymoron; spontaneous means unplanned.

> What a wonderful life I've had! I only wish I'd realized it sooner.
>
> — *Colette*

Being spontaneous also means allowing more chance in your life. The more chance you let in your world, the more interesting your world will become. Let more people into your life. Communicate with them and express yourself to them, especially if they have a different viewpoint from your own. You might learn something new.

Remember to be spontaneous on a regular basis. Every day practice doing something that you haven't planned. On the spur of the moment, choose and do something new and exciting. It can be quite a small thing, like taking a different route somewhere, eating in a different restaurant, or going to some new kind of entertainment. You can make your life much more interesting by introducing something novel in all your activities.

> The only completely consistent people are the dead.
>
> — *Aldous Huxley*

Be a Creative Loafer and Be More Productive

An efficiency expert was hired by Henry Ford's company to examine the performance of the company. The expert's report was highly favorable, except for one employee who was regarded with great suspicion by the expert. The expert told Henry Ford, "That lazy man over in that office is wasting your money. Every time I go by that office he's just there sitting with his feet on his desk." Henry Ford replied, "That man once had an idea that saved us millions of dollars." Ford added, "At the time he had the idea, his feet were planted right where they are now — on that same desk."

Henry Ford defended the employee with his feet on the desk because he knew the value of creative loafers. These individuals are peak performers because they tend to be very productive and innovative in an optimal time frame. Creative loafers are certainly not workaholics; however, they are capable of hard work when the mood strikes or when it is necessary to do so. In the long run, these peak performers tend to be much more productive than workaholics.

> The formula for complete happiness is to be very busy with the unimportant.
>
> — A. Edward Newton

Throughout history there have been many highly creative people who were productive due to their ability to goof off or indulge in creative loafing. Mark Twain did most of his writing in bed. Samuel Johnson rarely rose before noon. Other highly creative individuals who were considered notorious layabouts include Oscar Wilde, Bertrand Russell, and Robert Louis Stevenson.

If you want to enhance the quality of your life, challenging your thinking about work and leisure is another good area on which to focus. Working long hours is supposed to be the key to success. Contrary to public belief, this is seldom the case. For some mysterious reason, people who espouse the virtues of hard work in our society overlook the fact that several million people keep their noses to the grindstone throughout their careers and wind up with nothing but flat noses. They certainly don't fulfill their dreams.

> They intoxicate themselves with work so they won't see how they really are.
>
> — Aldous Huxley

The Economist, in 1996, reported that, although overwork is common in North America, at least some companies are starting to see the light and are resisting it. For example, Hewlett-Packard has started a campaign to persuade its 100,000 workers to have a better balance between work and play, by asking what value a task will bring and what will happen if employees don't do it. Susan Moriconi, head of the company's Work/Life Program, states that long hours and unnecessary business trips reduce creativity and wear down employees emotionally and physically.

Most people haven't stopped to consider that a great deal of harm may result from the belief that hard work is a virtue. Although work is necessary for our survival, working long hours doesn't contribute as much to individual well-being as many think it does.

How to Leisure Your Life Away

Living the moment is extremely important for mastering the art of handling your leisure time. Leisure is supposed to be easy for us to handle, on weekends and when we retire. Nothing is further from the truth. We are socialized to work hard and to feel guilty about not working. Many people are afraid of free time, or just plain don't know how to enjoy it. Some researchers say most Americans don't want more leisure time; they only get meaning and satisfaction from doing things.

Discipline and a certain attitude are required to utilize leisure time wisely. To be a connoisseur of leisure, you must regularly stop and smell the roses. Leisure should transcend just being a time to rest for the sake of one's work. True leisure time is spent at activities such as intimate conversation, tennis, sex, or watching a sunset; it is for the sake of enjoying the activity itself. True leisure is anything that is done for sheer pleasure, and not so one can be more productive at work.

If you can't think of any leisure activities to enjoy, you are working too hard and haven't spent enough time getting to know yourself. It is never too late for you to develop a new interest or learn a new sport or skill. Start by writing down the things that you would like to pursue in your life before you die. Your list may be based on things you like doing now, things you loved doing in the past but have quit doing, and things you thought about doing but have never tried. Think of all the things that you love in life; then, in some way relate them to leisure activities that you can pursue. Here is a list created by the British writer Agatha Christie (1890–1976), as included in the book *Agatha Christie: An Autobiography*. This list may trigger some of the things that turn you on.

Creativity Principle:

Be Spontaneous

- Sunshine
- Apples
- Almost any kind of music
- Railway trains
- Numerical puzzles and anything to do with numbers
- Going to the sea
- Bathing and swimming
- Silence
- Sleeping
- Dreaming
- Eating
- The smell of coffee
- Lilies of the valley
- Most dogs
- Going to the theater

If people really liked to work, we'd still be plowing the land with sticks and transporting goods on our backs.
— *William Feather*

Note that quality leisure is dependent upon being engaged in at least a few active activities that involve risk and challenge. Passive activities, such as watching television and shopping, won't provide much satisfaction. Examples of active activities are reading, writing, exercising, taking a course, and learning a new language. Because these activities involve some risk and challenge, they are more enjoyable and satisfying.

The quality of your life will depend on how you utilize your leisure time. Being your own person means that you get to choose how you utilize your leisure time so that it reflects your individuality and personality. You get to choose your own schedule without having to compromise for someone else's likes and dislikes. Using your leisure time wisely ensures that you will keep growing and learning as you venture through the different phases of life. Don't forget about life's simple pleasures. If you're feeling bored or lonely, then

> Work is the refuge of people who have nothing better to do.
>
> — *Oscar Wilde*

- Visit the local coffee bar and watch the people.
- Have a heart-to-heart conversation with a six-year-old.
- Go for a two-hour walk in the park.
- Take a nap.
- Do something unreasonable.
- Plan a party and invite many interesting people.
- Walk barefoot through a stream.
- Read Jane Austen or Danielle Steele down by the river.
- Attend a concert.
- Take up a new sport just for the fun of it.
- Look at the beauty of nature all around you.
- Treat yourself to a minivacation.
- Start writing your book.
- Spend the entire day in a park just watching people.
- Watch children and pets at play.
- Phone an old friend whom you haven't talked to for awhile.

> If hard work was such a wonderful thing, the rich would have kept it all to themselves.
>
> — *Lane Kirkland*

Be sure to seek out new people, new places, and new points of view. The unknown and unexpected will add to your experience of life. Activities such as music, gardening, meditating, and taking a walk in the park can be spiritual in nature. Risk, experiment, and don't forget to have some fun while you are at it. Generate the creative energy to continue in a positive manner, regardless of which negative events seem to conspire against you. Find reasons to do the important things, instead of not to do them.

Eat, Drink, and Be Merry, Because Tomorrow We Die

My personal hobbies are reading, listening to music, and silence.

— *Dame Edith Sitwell*

Opting out of the rat race, and putting more leisure time into your days, can lead to a far richer life. Less can be more. It takes courage and trust in one's intuition to make a dramatic change in one's life, and to forego security and a great deal of money in the process. Here is the contents of a letter that I received from Rita in Vancouver, who decided to take a sabbatical from work by quitting her job.

> Dear Mr. Zelinski:
>
> I have just finished reading your book *The Joy of Not Working* (yes, I did all the exercises too). I love it! Congratulations on a fantastic book.
>
> I had been teaching seven days a week, six to twelve hours a day without a holiday at a music school for the last twelve years. I originally took the job to earn my way through my Commerce degree, but I continued to habitually work after my graduation five years ago.
>
> The job was ruining my life — so I "retired" (after all, I'm still in my twenties) two months ago. Although I was happy with my decision, I was not prepared for my new lifestyle. My friends and colleagues severely criticized me, and I had to find new ways to spend my extra time.
>
> Having read your book, I am convinced that I made the right decision. I am now even proud to be not working.
>
> Yours truly,
>
> Rita

CALVIN AND HOBBES

I had the opportunity to talk to Rita about six months after she wrote to me. Her sabbatical from the workplace had done her a lot of good. She said that she was back at work, but working fewer hours, enjoying herself more, and being more productive.

You can bring your life under control and put it in better balance by reorienting yourself to a new relationship with leisure. By deciding to be a peak performer with a healthy balance between work and play, instead of a workaholic, you will have more fun in life. Remember that you may be undermining your life if you are spending too much time at work and little time in leisure activities. Community life and the quality of your work will also suffer. Also keep in mind that you don't know anyone who on his or her deathbed said, "I wish I would have worked more."

> We work to become, not to acquire.
>
> — Elbert Hubbard

Being fully alive means being able to experience the moment. Life will take on a more exciting quality when you learn how to be more leisurely and conscious of the moment. Being in the here and now is learning to pay attention to the world around you so you have control over the important events in your life. Experiencing the now in your leisure activities will mean each day will be enhanced with richness and intrigue.

> Work is what you do so that some time you won't have to do it anymore.
>
> — Alfred Polgar

Leisure activities provide unlimited opportunities for growth and satisfaction. As a creative individual, you should have the ability and freedom to find the time to pursue constructive leisure activities. The big advantage of being creative is you get to design your work schedule, your leisure time, your friendships, and your relationships, for a lifestyle that is truly your own.

Don't spend your time dreaming and fantasizing about how much better things would be if only you were in a relationship, made more money, or had a better job. The importance of living the moment should be as clear to you as a Zen master's moment of truth. If you postpone the chance to live life, it may slip away altogether. The time to start living is now. As the wise person said, "Eat, drink, and be merry, because tomorrow we die."

> When pleasure interferes with business, give up business.
>
> — Unknown Wise Person

Creativity Is a Three-Letter Word

Why You Must Become A Quick-Change Artist

In the preceding chapters we looked at principles that I consider vital for our creative success. These are principles that, if followed regularly, can make a big difference in our lives. Even by using these principles infrequently, we have a chance to impact substantially upon our lives and those of others.

The question is, "Is our success in our careers assured if we follow all the creativity principles?" Before I answer that, first let us look at the world as it looks today. Following are the conditions that reflect the modern world, the climate that everyone has to deal with; we have virtually no choice about whether or not we can escape these conditions.

- Intense and accelerating change
- Unpredictable events
- Unstable and chaotic conditions
- Impact of high technology
- Downsizing and cutbacks
- Powerful consumer forces
- Global economy

> You think you understand the situation, but what you don't understand is that the situation has just changed.
>
> — *Financial Advertisement*

Welcome to the exciting end of the 1990s and the start of the new millennium. No individual can take anything for granted in the workplace. Change is not only rapid, but accelerating at an intense pace.

People felt the start of the early 1990s was a time of rapid change. The rate of change of the early 1990s now looks like a snail's pace (and a piece of cake) in comparison to the rate of change at the end of the 1990s. As we approach the start of the new millennium, we can expect the rate of change to increase at a greater rate than the late 1990s. What this means is, there is but one certainty in today's world: If you still haven't noticed, today the only certainty is uncertainty.

> The more unpredictable the world becomes, the more we rely on predictions.
> — *Steve Rivkin*

You must become a quick-change artist to deal with the shape of the modern world. Just look at the recent headlines in national publications such as the *Globe & Mail, USA TODAY,* and *Fortune.* You will read "How Safe Is Your Job?"; "Shrinking Possibilities for Architects"; "The Pain of Downsizing"; "Why So Many Managers Are Quitting Corporate America to Strike Out on Their Own"; "What's Happening to Jobs in America"; and "How the New Executive Unemployed Are Coping." Looking at these headlines confirms that uncertainty is the one thing we can count on in the workplace; beyond this there are no guarantees.

So even if we follow all the creativity principles in this book, our success isn't certain. Then why should we follow and apply these principles and techniques? Simply because our chances for creative success are increased many times when we persist in following these principles. Being persistent in being creative will have its payoffs on most, if not all, projects we undertake.

> The only modern fairy tale is the one that begins: Once upon a time, there was a secure job.
> — *Unknown Wise Person*

As a quick-change artist, you will be able to adapt to the shape of things to come. To deal effectively with today's unprecedented pace, your opinions, beliefs, and values shouldn't be carved in stone. Avoid being a rigid person, and your life will be a lot easier in the new world. Some people think changing values, beliefs, or opinions represents weakness. On the contrary, the ability to change represents strength and a willingness to grow.

There is much to be said for the saying that only the foolish and dead never change their beliefs and opinions. As I implied before, no matter who you are, you can change. I want to stress that the more inflexible and less perceptual you are, the more problems you will have in living and adjusting to our rapidly changing world.

As stated in the preface, my experience in teaching creativity semi-nars reveals that people who most need to change their thinking are most resistant to change. The opposite is true with highly adaptive and creative people. To them, change is exciting. They are always willing to challenge their points of view, and they are willing to change them when necessary.

Never challenging our points of view to see if they are still valid has at least two inherent dangers:

- The first danger is we may get locked into one way of thinking, without seeing other alternatives that may be more appropriate.

- The second danger is we may adopt a set of values that at the time make a lot of sense. Time will pass; with time, things will change. The original values will no longer be appropriate, because of the changes, but we will still continue to function with the original, outmoded values.

The new millennium will be frustrating and unrewarding for those who choose not to use their creative abilities. For those who develop their creative skills and persist in using them, the times will offer many opportunities. The future belongs to those who will learn how to cope with and thrive on uncertainty. People who have learned to think laterally, search for many solu-tions, look for the obvious, take risks, celebrate failure, fully explore all ideas, and like chaos will be at the forefront of business. They will be the people making a difference as entrepreneurs in their own businesses or as leaders of the progressive organizations of the new world.

> It's what you learn after you know it all that counts.
> — *John Wooden*

A New Paradigm for Success

I have found that some people embrace my books for all the wrong rea-sons; I trust that you won't do the same. Thomas Carlyle said, "The best effect of any book is that it excites the reader to self-activity." I hope that this book will have opened a new way of life for you. Now is the time to take all the important material that is relevant to your life and "run with it." I hope you will be motivated in some way to undertake some of the difficult things in the short term, so that your life becomes easier in the long term. As you have learned by now, life isn't easy. However, by fol-lowing the seventeen creativity principles of this book, it isn't that diffi-cult to create a rewarding life at work and at play.

Some people will think this book is a book on how to become rich and famous. Creative success doesn't mean being rich and famous. If you aren't receiving satisfaction from your life and you think that fame and fortune are what will get you there, you will require nothing short of a paradigm shift to get you on the right track. A paradigm is a belief or explanation of some situation that a group of people share. A shift from an old paradigm to a new paradigm is a distinctive, new way of thinking about old problems.

If you want to hear about the power and glory of wealth, ask a man who's seeking it. But if you want to learn of wealth's burdens and difficulties, ask a man who's been wealthy a long time.

— Stanley Goldstein

Your paradigm shift should involve a change of your beliefs about success. Success is possible without being rich or famous. Success peddled by society means a high-paying job, celebrity status, a big home, and a luxury car. This isn't the only way to define success; success can be defined in many ways. With a paradigm shift, success takes on a different meaning.

Truly creative, successful people show a concern for the world around them. Their focus is not just on themselves and their career or business but also on the environment, the poor, the disadvantaged, and the need for world peace.

Today being an entrepreneur has become a goal for many. If you want to be an entrepreneur because it will bring you fame and fortune, you ain't no genuine entrepreneur. As a true entrepreneur you should be looking at how you are making the world a better place to live for yourself and others. The satisfaction you will receive from making a modest living selling a product that enhances the lives of other people is tenfold over the satisfaction you will receive if you make lots of money from something not that beneficial to the world, such as being involved in a pyramid scheme or selling contraband cigarettes.

"I Don't Want To Be the Richest Man in the Graveyard"

— Song by Ben Kerr

Vince Lombardi's "winning is the only thing" also shouldn't be construed as the only success. Some people consider the players with Buffalo Bills of the National Football League "losers" because they lost the Superbowl four years in a row. How many other NFL football teams have appeared in the Superbowl four years in a row? This team is one of the most successful ever, and many bubbleheads are calling its players "losers."

It is always hard to resist thinking of a successful person as someone who is rich and famous. Fame and fortune are okay as a bonus in life, but they aren't essential for having lived creatively and productively. The obsession with fame and fortune indicates shortcomings in the values common in North America. If you have adopted these values, you may want to consider seeing things differently. Having strict beliefs that fame and fortune are necessary for happiness and success will leave you dissatisfied and unfulfilled.

The following letter, sent to me from a man who had read *The Joy of Not Working*, shows the power of rediscovering one's creativity for a purpose other than fame and fortune.

> Mr. Zelinski:
>
> Your book *The Joy of Not Working* pinpointed many of the things that are wrong with our society, such as materialism and the crazy attitude we have toward work. But what impressed me the most was how you stressed that people should use their creativity and imagination to get more out of life.
>
> After reading the book I began to look at my life in a much different way. To my surprise I found a creative side of me that I never knew existed. I just spent the last year writing a book and I have never felt so good about accomplishing something. So good that I just had to write you. Throughout the writing, my motto has always been straight from page 138: "If your book is enjoyed by one person other than yourself, it is a success — anything over and above this is a bonus."
>
> Respectively,
>
> N. K.

Whether it is writing or learning to play a piano for a greater purpose than just to make money at it, a creative outlet will help confirm your creativity. Being a creative thinker allows you to see that modifying your values for a more modest emphasis on fame and materialism has its merits. Here's something to think about: No matter how rich and popular you become in your life, the number of people at your funeral will depend upon the weather.

> Success for some people, depends on becoming well known, for others it depends on never being found out.
>
> — *Ashleigh Brilliant*

Look Inside If You Want to Find More Outside

All individuals can make their lives worthwhile and satisfying by being more creative and enjoying the many pleasures that life offers. What individuals require for success is an important mission or purpose, high self-esteem, a good attitude, and the ability to enjoy leisure time. Much of this book has focused on the external world. We can achieve a certain degree of happiness in this world by reaching outward. Working at an interesting job, playing tennis, socializing with friends and acquaintances, traveling to exotic destinations, and going to the opera can give us a certain amount of pleasure in life. However, we must not forget the pleasures available to us when we cultivate our inner selves. The external world will offer only occasional and sporadic pleasures, if we haven't taken time to develop our spiritual selves. To get more out of the external world, we must tune into the inner world.

To paint a fine picture is far more important than to sell it.

— Edward Alden Jewell

The spiritual self, probably the most important element for a rewarding life once our basic necessities have been satisfied, is usually the most neglected, ignored, or denied by people in our materialistically oriented society. Many individuals are looking for something external to fill a void that can only be filled by developing a rich inner world. Society teaches us to value materialistic things and to ignore the intangible inner resources we all possess. The easy life is supposed to be just around the corner with the arrival of a new job, a big lottery win, or a new marriage partner. Desperate, externally oriented individuals want certain things so badly that they often drive these things away from themselves. They are looking for a savior as an outside source, when in fact, the savior is an inside source. Outer-directed individuals are at the mercy of societal judgment, which serves to limit opportunities for personal growth and development.

Taoism, like most religions, teaches us that when we look within ourselves, we find all that we need to make our lives happy and fulfilling. By searching within, we achieve clarity; life becomes effortless because we gain simplicity. Taoism stresses that simplicity is the ultimate expression of personal power. The inner world is the foundation for self-confidence and self-worth.

It is those of us who have a deep and real inner life who are best able to deal with the irritating details of outer life.

— Evelyn Underhill

Internal orientation may not sound important to individuals in their teens or early twenties, but this is an essential ingredient for self-development as we grow older. The spiritual self is attained through much higher levels of consciousness than those used in sports, entertainment, or working. Well-balanced singles aren't at the mercy of the external world, because they have taken the time to develop a rich internal world.

The inner world holds the key to life filled with joy, satisfaction, and happiness. Committing yourself to the inner life and the voice within will result in strength and confidence not available in the outer world. The way to escape loneliness and despair is to develop your spirituality. Self-development can be mysterious, but it is also wondrous and fascinating. Self-questioning and personal growth result in self-determination, which brings greater freedom. You must look inside, if you want to find more outside.

Highly Creative People Never Soar Too High

If you look at creative people, you will see they have success at work and play. Here are the traits of the highly creative who have a good balance in their lives.

Creative people are different. Most people spend their time trying to fit in with the rest of society. They conform because they are approval seekers and don't want to stand out. Creative people have no problem being different. They stand out. Whether at work or at play, they don't care what others think. They do not let society dictate how they should behave. They won't engage in small talk because it is the proper and polite thing to do. To the creative, conformity is dull and interferes with one's ability to do the new and rewarding. Because creative people aren't approval seekers, they have more freedom to pursue leisure activities that contribute to personal growth and satisfaction.

> It's better to be a lion for a day than a sheep all your ife.
> — *Sister Elizabeth Kenny*

Creative people are comfortable with change and uncertainty. In today's chaotic world creative people, whether at work or at play, welcome change and aren't threatened by uncertainty. With change comes an opportunity to learn and grow. People who know how to use their creative abilities are the ones who are not only coping with but thriving on the chaos in the modern world.

Creative people are enthusiastic about life. Enthusiasm is different from excitement. Excitement is an occasional outburst of energy or joy, but enthusiasm is an internal energy that flows from one's essence. Creative people have taken the time to develop an essence and a rich internal world. They project a constant zest for living and don't have to rely on outside influences to excite them. Although unenthusiastic people display occasional excitement from external stimulants, they have little zest for life. Creative people are capable of enjoying television, parties, nightclubs, taverns, and the like, but you won't find them spending too much time with these. Instead, you will find them enjoying more rewarding activities, ones that unenthusiastic people miss out on.

Creative people are self-motivated, with defined goals. They set goals that they work toward. Goals give them a purpose. To achieve these goals requires motivation. Because creative people are doers, they don't have to go and hear motivational speakers like unmotivated people do. They are self-directed enough to just go out and do it. When creative

BIZARRO

people lose jobs, and along with it their purpose, they create another purpose. The new purpose is as important — or more important — than the one they had in a career or a job.

Creative people can enjoy themselves when alone. These individuals don't always have to be with people. They relish being alone regularly. Their motto is, "It is better to be alone than in bad company." Because they aren't overly dependent on people, they develop a few quality friendships rather than a lot of superficial ones. To them, aloneness is not synonymous with loneliness. They know that people who always have to be with others are some of the loneliest people around. Creative people not only enjoy being alone, they often demand their privacy. They have a rich inner world to complement their rich outer world. Their ability to be alone makes it easy for them to have a satisfying time when other people are just not available to be with them. Yet you will find creative people to be some of the most sociable people around.

Creative people experience freedom from failure. They know how to fail; they do not view failure in the same way as the majority. Failure, to creative people, is a means to success. They realize that the best way to double their success rate is to double their failure rate. To be successful in one's career, a person must have had many set-backs. There is no difference in achieving success in one's life of leisure. Only by having experienced regular failure will one have achieved a great deal of success.

No bird soars too high, if he soars with his own wings.
— *William Blake*

Creative people are adventurous. They like to explore the world around them. They like to travel to new destinations, to meet new people, and to see new things. Being moderate risk takers, they will try activities with an element of danger. Naturally curious, creative people want to learn every present moment of their lives. There are unlimited opportunities for doing, thinking, feeling, loving, laughing, and living.

It is obvious from the above traits of creative people that your positive attitude about life is the most important trait you can possess. By shaping your own attitude, you make life what it is. No one but you gets to make your own bed. No one but you can ever put in the effort to make your life work. No one but you can generate the joy, the enthusiasm, or the motivation to live your life to the fullest.

Thinking for a Change

You should have noticed by now that creative living is more than just having a "great idea." Now you must do something with what you have learned. Activity and inner mobility will go a long way. You have to love the world to be of service to it. Always try to seek growth, not perfection. You are the creator of the context in which you view things. It is up to you to find a way to enjoy the activities you undertake. Let your interests be as wide as possible; the variety in life makes the effort to experience that variety well worthwhile.

> Any powerful idea is absolutely fascinating and absolutely useless until we choose to use it.
> — *Richard Bach*

Looking past your present beliefs and perceptions may open up many new dimensions to living. Develop a presence of mind to question everything you believe. Learn to weed out old, unworkable beliefs. At the same time, develop the ability to adopt new values and fresh behaviors to see whether they are workable. By challenging and changing your thinking, you set the stage for fresh perspectives and new values to replace outmoded beliefs.

We can change the quality of our lives by changing the context in which we view our circumstances. Two people can be faced with the same situation, such as being fired from a job, yet one will view it as a blessing, and the other will view it as a curse. Changing the context of the situation depends on our ability to challenge and be flexible in our thinking. Most of us do not take the time to reflect upon what we are thinking and why. To produce change in our thinking, we must start thinking for a change.

By challenging and changing your thinking, you set the stage for fresh perspectives and new values to replace outmoded beliefs. The question you should ask yourself is, "Do I want to 'think for a change' and make a creative difference in my life and the lives of others?"

Once you have decided you want to make a difference in this world, you must be committed to making that difference. Don't be a carbon copy; instead, be an original. Take the time to think about how you are limiting yourself in your life by trying to be like everyone else. If you have an unhealthy need to always fit in and be accepted by everyone, you are setting yourself up for a life of boredom. In addition, chances are others will find you rather boring. In other words, if you want your life to be boring, then conform and be dull; if you want your life to be interesting and exciting, then be different.

> There is only one success — to be able to spend your life in your own way.
>
> — *Christopher Morley*

You are the only person who can choose for you to be creative. You are the only person who can do the work that needs to be done. You are the only person who can supply the energy, the enthusiasm, the courage, the unreasonableness, the spontaneity, the discipline, and the persistence that is required. Your life will be as adventurous, exciting, and rewarding as you want it to be.

Today's world is filled with an infinite number of possibilities for using the principles from this book. You must remember to refrain from being a know-it-all. In experiencing the joy of not knowing it all, you must also remember this: Creativity is not society. Creativity is not your organization. Creativity is not your education. Creativity is not your intelligence. And creativity is not your knowledge. Just what is creativity? Creativity is your natural ability to think in new and wonderful ways and make a big difference in this world.

Creativity is a three-letter word. Creativity is _____! (For the one and only right answer to this, see Appendix, page 182.)

Appendix

Solutions to Exercises

Exercise 1–1.
How to make an egg stand on its end:
Columbus and the Eggheads

- Use some glue.
- Use some gum.
- Put some salt on the table.
- Use an egg holder.
- Use a nail.
- Gently tap an unboiled egg until the shell is slightly broken, and you will have no trouble standing it on its end.
- Wait until the equinox and stand the egg on its end using the electromagnetic forces.
- With a pen write *end* on the side of the egg, then lay the egg on the side where *end* is written, and you have the egg standing on its "end."

Exercise 1–2. What do a book, bed, and beer have in common?

- All are represented by words that, spelled backward, make no sense.
- All of them put you to sleep.
- All can be found in most hotel rooms.
- If dropped from a high-rise apartment, all can be damaged.
- Fish don't normally need any of them.

- All can be bought in a shopping mall.
- You don't have to be an intellectual to enjoy any of them.
- All have been stolen.
- All can be imagined.
- You can't take any of them with you when you die.
- All have been given as gifts.
- All can be enjoyed alone.
- All can be used to enhance sex (if you are creative).
- All have been used in making movies.
- David Letterman has talked about all three on his show.
- All can be purchased for under $1,000.
- All have been used in one way or another to make money.
- All have got people in trouble. (book — *Satanic Verses*)
- All are not standard equipment on a Rolls Royce.
- All have a lot in common with a boot.
- They all don't have a lot in common with pigeons.
- When frozen, all three are solids.

Exercise 2-3. The Old "Nine into Six" Trick

Add the line as shown above and turn the page upside down to get VI.

Exercise 2-4. The "Classic" Nine-Circle Exercise
Part A

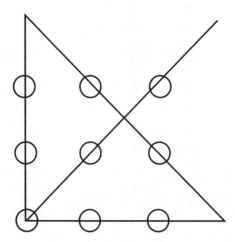

Part B

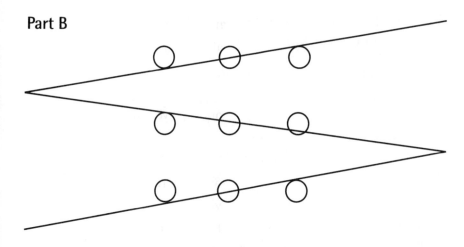

Part C

This part has at least seven different solutions. One is to cut out the nine circles with a pair of scissors and line them up. Then draw a straight line through them. Another solution is to use a very wide line.

Exercise 4-4. Playing with Matches (b)

1. Move one of the matchsticks from the II to get **III + I = IV**. (Note that, since either matchstick can be moved, this constitutes two solutions.)

2. Move one of the matchsticks from the III to get **II + II = IV**. (This translates into three solutions, since either of three matchsticks can be moved.)

3. Move the vertical matchstick from IV to get **III + II = V**.

4. Move one of the matchsticks from the V to get **IIII - II = II**. (The last matchstick remains slanted.)

5. Move the matchstick from the minus sign to get **IIIIII = IV**. Now look at this in the mirror, which reads **VI = IIIIII**. To make both sides equal, count the number of matchsticks on the right side of the equation, which gives **VI = six**.

6. Take the vertical matchstick from IV, break it in half, and then use the halves to create **-III - II = -V**.

7. Take one of the matchsticks from the V and light it up. Then burn the remaining one from the V and throw the first lit one away to end up with **III-II = I**.

8. Move one of the matchsticks from the III over the equal sign to end up with **II - II ≠ IV**.

Exercise 6-3. The Advantages (and Disadvantages) of Drinking on the Job

Plus	Minus	Interesting
• People will be more creative.	• Safety goes down.	• What would happen if we allowed drinking on special occasions?
• Employees want to come to work.	• More people falling asleep	• How many people would actually drink on the job?
• Better communication	• Productivity goes down.	
• Great way to find out who the alcoholics are	• Need more washrooms	
• Good way to make extra revenue for the company	• More affairs (This could be a plus as well.)	
	• Could lead to fights	

Exercise 8-7. The Graffiti Puzzle

The truck owner had taken some paint and modified the Graffiti to read

FORD

Exercise 8-9. Easy to Miss the Boat

The man is Chinese because his mother and father were.

Chapter 9 - Mind Bender 2

The prime minister bought the numbers two and four for the address on his house.

Chapter 9 – Rebus Exercises

Ha! I bet you thought this was going be easy. To make it a little more difficult, I have mixed up the solutions.

bad spell of the flu

scatter brain

Times Square

drawing on my knowledge

inequality of the sexes

paradigm shift

time out

missing man

I see you are creative

inclined to be honest

part-time

being on time

split decision

about turn

mixed signals

salary gap

triple play

U-turn

divided factions

they are after me

shattered dreams

see-through blouse

black eye

afternoon tea

miscalculation

equal rights

whitewash

reverse logic

I am under the gun

toy box

long weekend

unfinished business

elevator going up

parachutes

freeways

way up

Exercise 12–1. Abbreviations to Elongate Your Mind

1. This was supposed to stand for "four pair equals eight." However, a former girlfriend of mine gave her second answer to this as "Foreplay is essential."

2. *J* stands for Jaguar.

3. *F* stands for foot.

4. *E* stands for east.

5. *N* stands for north.

6. *A* stands for America.

7. *C* stands for century.

8. *Z* stands for zero.

9. *S* stands for San.

10. *R* stands for Ronald.

11. *Y* stands for your.

12. *S* stands for saved.

13. *U* stands for up.

14. *Y* stands for year.

15. *R* stands for rolling.

16. *W* stands for wife.

17. *D* stands for day.

18. *S* stands for saw.

19. *D* stands for day.

20. *P* stands for Post.

21. *P* stands for Paul.

22. *Y* stands for year.

23. *M* stands for Madonna.

24. *N* stands for New.

25. *M* stands for months.

Exercise 13-1. Twice as Fishy but Just as Square

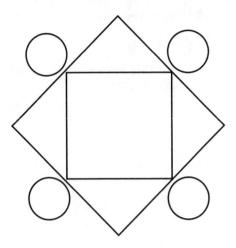

Exercise 13-3. Breaking the Chain of Demand

Only two links need be cut. If the businessman cuts only the seventh and eleventh links, he will have two single links, and one chain each of three links, six links, and twelve links. With these it is possible for the businessman to increase his payment of one link a day for twenty-three days. For example, on the fifth day he will give the two single links and the chain of three links.

Chapter 16 – Page 176

Bibliography and Recommended Books on Creativity

Bach, Richard. *Illusions: The Adventures of a Reluctant Messiah.* New York: Dell, 1977.

Buzan, Tony, and Barry Buzan. *The Mind Map Book.* New York: NAL-Dutton, 1994.

De Bono, Edward. *Lateral Thinking.* New York: HarperCollins, 1990.
——————. *Six Thinking Hats.* New York: Little Brown, 1986.

Buchman, Dian Dincin, and Seli Groves. *What If? Fifty Discoveries That Changed the World.* New York: Scholastic, 1988.

Flatow, Ira. *They All Laughed.* New York: HarperCollins, 1993.

Gawain, Shakti. *Living in the Light.* New York: Bantam, 1993.

Goleman, Daniel, Paul Kaufman, and Michael Ray. *The Creative Spirit.* New York: NAL-Dutton, 1993.

Hank, Kurt, and Jay Parry. *Wake Up Your Creative Genius.* Menlo Park, California: Crisp Publications, 1991.

Koberg, Don, and Jim Bagnall. *The Universal Traveler.* Menlo Park, California: Crisp Publications, 1991.

Kriegel, Robert J., and Louis Patler. *If It Ain't Broke . . . Break It!* New York: Warner Books, 1992.

LeBoeuf, Michael. *Imagineering — How to Profit from Your Creative Powers.* New York: Berkley Publishing Group, 1986.

Miller, William C. *The Creative Edge.* Reading, Massachusetts: Addison-Wesley, 1989.

Nierenberg, Gerald I. *The Art of Creative Thinking.* New York: Simon & Schuster, 1982.

Nolan, Vincent. *Problem Solving.* London: Sphere Books, 1987.

Ray, Michael, and Rochelle Myers. *Creativity in Business.* New York: Doubleday & Co., 1989.

Raudsepp, Eugene. *Growth Games for the Creative Manager.* New York: Perigee Books, 1987.

Saint Exupéry, Antoine de. *The Little Prince.* San Diego, California: Harcourt, Brace, Jovanovich, Inc., 1988.

Sher, Barbara. *Wishcraft: How to Get What You Really Want.* New York: Delacorte Press, 1994.

Shock, Robert L. *Why Didn't I Think of That?* New York: New American Library Books, 1982.

Thompson, Charles. *What a Great Idea!* New York: HarperCollins, 1992.

Thompson, Charles, and Lael Lyons. *"Yes, But . . ." The Top Forty Killer Phrases and How to Fight Them.* New York: Harper Business, 1994.

Torrance, Paul. *The Search for Satori & Creativity.* New York: Creative Education Foundation & Creative Synergetic Associates, 1979.

Van Gundy, Arthur B. *Training Your Creative Mind.* East Aurora, New York: Beally Ltd., 1991.

Von Oech, Roger. *A Kick in the Seat of the Pants.* New York: HarperCollins, 1986.

—————. *A Whack on the Side of the Head.* New York: Warner Books, 1993.

Waitley, Denis E. *Winning the Innovation Game.* New York: Berkley Publishing Group, 1989.

Ernie Zelinski is a consultant and professional speaker in the field of applying creativity to business and leisure. He is the author of *The Joy of Not Working*, which has taught over 50,000 people about living every part of their lives—work and play, employment, unemployment, and retirement alike—to the fullest. Ernie lives in Edmonton, Alberta, Canada, where, besides just hanging around his favorite coffee bars, he enjoys cycling, tennis, reading, and traveling:

The author would be pleased to hear from his readers. If you have any questions or comments, please write directly to

Ernie Zelinski
P. O. Box 4072
Edmonton, Alberta
Canada T6E 4S8

Ernie Zelinski is available as a keynote speaker and seminar presenter in the areas of creativity and leisure. For more information, please contact Visions International Presentations at (403) 436-1798.